21 CANDLESTICKS
EVERY TRADER
SHOULD KNOW

21 CANDLESTICKS EVERY TRADER SHOULD KNOW

DR. MELVIN PASTERNAK

MARKETPLACE BOOKS®
COLUMBIA, MARYLAND

This book, along with other books, is available at discounts that make it realistic to provide them as gifts to your customers, clients, and staff. For more information on these long lasting, cost effective premiums, please call us at 800-272-2855 or e-mail us at sales@traderslibrary.com.

ISBN 1-59280-298-2

Printed in the United States of America.

1 2 3 4 5 6 7 8 9 10

CONTENTS

PREFACE

J apanese Candlesticks are one of the most powerful technical analysis tools in the trader's toolkit. While candlestick charts date back to Japan in the 1700's, this form of charting did not become popular in the Western world until the early 1990's. Since that time, they have become the default mode of charting for serious technical analysts, replacing the open-high-low-close bar chart.

Because of this surge in popularity, there has been a great deal of cogent information published on candlestick charting both in book form and on the worldwide Web. Many of the works, however, are encyclopedic in nature. There are perhaps 100 individual candlesticks and candle patterns that are presented: a daunting amount of information for a trader to learn.

In this book, I have selected 21 candles that I believe every trader should know by name. These are the candles that in my experience occur most frequently and have the greatest relevance for helping you make trading decisions. Just as knowing the name of a person helps you immediately recognize them on a crowded street; so being able to name the candlestick allows you to pick it out of a chart pattern. Being able to name it allows you to appreciate its technical implications and increases the accuracy of your predictions.

In my trading, I try to integrate candlestick analysis, moving averages, Bollinger bands, price patterns (such as triangles), and indicators such as stochastics or CCI to reach decisions. I find that the more information that is integrated, the more likely it is that the decision will be correct. In this book, I have chosen to combine moving averages, Bollinger bands, and two indicators—stochastics, and CCI—on various charts. As we discuss individual candlesticks or candle patterns, I will integrate these tools. Hopefully, you will learn not only how to recognize candles, but also appreciate how you can combine them with the traditional tools of technical analysis.

In this book, my focus is on minor trend reversals: those of most interest to a trader. The minor trend typically lasts 5 to 15 days although, on occasion, I have seen it stretch out to about 30 trading days. These same candle principles also work equally well on 5-minute or weekly charts. It is simply a matter of adapting this information to the time frame in which you are trading.

Candles are your personal sentry providing you with consistent early warnings of impending trend change. They provide the earliest signal I know of that the patterns in the market are about to reverse.

WHAT YOU SHOULD KNOW ABOUT CANDLESTICKS

CANDLESTICKS ANTICIPATE, INDICATORS FOLLOW, AND TRENDLINES CONFIRM

I call candlesticks an anticipatory indicator. You haven't come across this wording before because it is my own terminology. An anticipatory indicator gives a signal in advance of other market action—in other words, it is a leading indicator of market activity.

Momentum indicators such as CCI (Commodity Channel Index) or stochastics are also anticipatory, because momentum usually precedes price. Typically, however, even rapidly moving momentum indicators such as CCI lag the candle signal by a day or two. When you receive a candle signal followed by a momentum signal such as stochastics, which communicates the same message, it is likely that in combination they are accurately predicting what will happen with a stock.

On the other hand, the break of a trendline or a moving average crossover is what I call a "confirming" signal. It usually occurs days after the peak or bottom of price and much after the candlestick and indicator signal.

Depending on your trading style, you can act on the anticipatory signal. However, if you prefer to be cautious and wait for more evidence, candlesticks anticipate a change in trend and alert you that a reversal may be imminent. In this case, you use candlesticks to confirm other indicators.

HOW TO READ A CANDLESTICK CHART

If you are already familiar with the basics of candlesticks, you can skim this section. If you have seen candles on the web, but have not studied them in some detail, then you'll now be given the background you need to use them.

Candles may be created for any "period" of chart—monthly, weekly, hourly, or even by minute. When I discuss candles in this book, I use daily chart examples: But be aware that you can create candle charts for virtually any period.

BAR VS. CANDLESTICK CHARTS

On the opposite page are a three-month bar chart and a three-month candlestick chart for IBM. See if you can spot any differences in the "data series."

Hard to spot the difference? That's because there isn't any. Both the bar chart and the candlestick chart contain exactly the same information, only presented in different form. Both the bar chart and the candle chart contain the same data: the high for the period (the day), the low, the open, and the close.

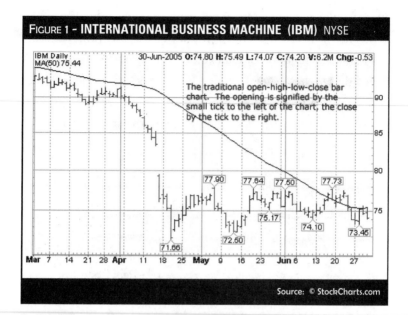

FIGURE 1 - **INTERNATIONAL BUSINESS MACHINE (IBM)** NYSE

The traditional open-high-low-close bar chart. The opening is signified by the small tick to the left of the chart, the close by the tick to the right.

Source: © StockCharts.com

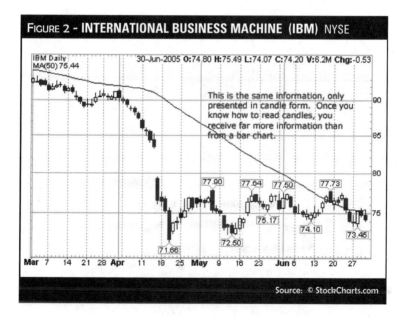

FIGURE 2 - **INTERNATIONAL BUSINESS MACHINE (IBM)** NYSE

This is the same information, only presented in candle form. Once you know how to read candles, you receive far more information than from a bar chart.

Source: © StockCharts.com

In a candlestick chart, however, the names are changed. The difference between the open and the close is called the *real body*. The amount the stock price moved higher beyond the real body is called the *upper shadow*. The amount the stock price moved lower is called the *lower shadow*. If the candle is clear or white it means the opening was lower than the high, and the stock went up. If the candle is colored, then the stock went down. This information is shown below:

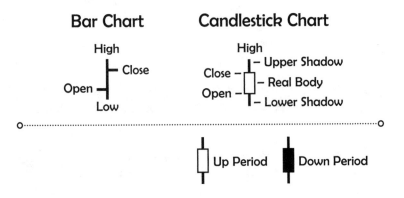

OPTIMISM AND PESSIMISM AS SHOWN BY CANDLES

Here is an idea about candlesticks that helps me use them better and which I haven't seen in books or on the Web.

It is generally acknowledged that the opening of the trading day is dominated by amateurs. The close, on the other hand, is dominated by professional traders. The low of the day, one might say, is set by the pessimists—they believed the market was going lower and sold at the bottom. The high of the day is set by the optimists. They were willing to pay top price but were incorrect in their analysis, at least in the short term.

Individual candlesticks may be understood by combining this concept with the candle chart. I will use only two examples, but you might want to experiment with this idea yourself.

Shaven Bottom/Shaven Head. The shaven bottom/shaven head candle depicts a day in which the market opened at the low and closed at the high. It is a day on which the amateurs are also the pessimists. They sell early and their shares are gobbled by eager buyers. By the end of the day, the optimists and professionals close the stock sharply higher. This bullish candle frequently predicts a higher open on the next day.

Shaven Bottom/Shaven Head

Shaven Head/Shaven Bottom. This candle is the opposite of the one just described. Depicted here is a day when the amateurs are the optimists. They buy at the top of the day, only to watch prices decline steadily. By the end of trading, prices have declined sharply and the professional pessimists are in control of the market. The opening the next day often is lower.

Shaven Head/Shaven Bottom

Candles can be understood better by reasoning them out in this way. Particularly when you see a candle with a large real body, ask yourself who won the battle of the day, the optimists or the pessimists, the amateurs or the professionals. This question will often provide you with an important clue to subsequent trading action.

ADVANTAGES OF CANDLE VS. BAR CHARTS

There are three major advantages of candlestick charts compared to bar charts.

1. Candlestick charts are much more "visually immediate" than bar charts. Once you get used to the candle chart, it is much easier to see what has happened for a specific period—be it a day, a week an hour or one minute.

With a bar chart you need to mentally project the price action. You need to say to yourself, "The left tick says that's where it opened, the right tick where it closed. Now I see. It was an up day." With a candlestick chart, it is done for you. You can spend your energy on analysis, not on figuring out what happened with the price.

2. With candles you can spot trends more quickly by seeing if the candles are clear or colored. Within a period of a trend, you can tell easily what a stock did in a specific period.

The candle makes it easier to spot large-range days. A large candlestick suggests something "dramatic" happened on that trading day. A small range day suggests there may be relative consensus on the share price. When I spot a large range day, I check the volume for that day as well. Was volume unusual? Was it, say, 50% higher than normal? If so, it is very likely that the large-range day may set the tone for many days afterward.

3. Most important, candles are vital for spotting reversals. These reversals are usually short term—precisely the kind the trader is looking for.

When traditional technical analysis talks about reversals, it is usually referring to formations that occur over long periods of time. Typical reversal patterns are the double top and head and shoulders. By definition, these involve smart money distributing their shares to naive traders and they normally occur over weeks or even months.

Candlesticks, however, are able to accurately pick up on the changes in trend which occur at the end of each short term swing in the market. If you pay meticulous attention to them, they often warn you of impending changes.

CANDLES ANTICIPATE SHORT TERM REVERSALS

The message of candlesticks is most powerful when the markets are at an extreme, that is when they are overbought or oversold. I define overbought as a market that has gone up too far too fast. Most of the buyers are in and the sellers are eager to nail down profits.

An oversold market, on the other hand, is one in which the sellers have been in control for several days or weeks. Prices have gone down too far too fast. Most of the traders who want to sell have done so and there are bargains—at least in the short term—to be had.

There are many overbought and oversold indicators, such as CCI, RSI (Relative Strength Index) and Williams' % R. However, one of the best is stochastics, which essentially measures the stock's price in relation to its range, usually over the past 14 periods. CCI typically agrees with stochastics and is useful for providing confirmation of its signal. I also almost always put a Bollinger Band on charts I analyze. John Bollinger created this tool to include 19 out of every 20 closing prices within the bands. Therefore, a close outside the band is significant. A close outside the upper band usually indicates the stock is overbought. When it is outside the lower band it is oversold.

When stochastics, CCI, and the Bollinger bands all agree, a stock or index is overbought or oversold, I take their alignment very seriously because there is a good chance a reversal is overdue. A significant candlestick tells me more exactly when the reversal might occur.

WHY CANDLESTICKS WORK

A chart may be viewed as a picture of the war between supply and demand. When a stock is moving up, the buyers are in control. There is more demand than supply. Purchasers are eager to acquire the stock and will pay up, hitting the ask price to do so. When a stock is declining, the reverse is true. Sellers are fearful and will not dicker over a few cents, being more likely to accept the bid. Candlesticks graphically show the balance between supply and demand. At key reversal junctures, this supply/demand equation shifts and is captured in the candle chart.

"THE RULE OF TWO"

Generally, no one candlestick should be judged in isolation. The general principle is that even if you see a key reversal candlestick, you should wait at least part of one more day before acting. If, for example, you spot a candle called a "doji," seek verification from the action of the next trading day. If there is a down gap and prices begin to decline, then it is prudent to take your position.

CANDLES IN ACTION: DOW JONES ANALYSIS

As stated in candlestick theory, there are many candles that signal important reversals. To conclude this section, we will focus on only four candlesticks that called every major turn in the Dow Jones Industrial Average over nearly a six month period! Think how much more accurately you could have traded the market if you knew these candles, names and implications and had recognized them when they occurred.

The good news is that these are reversal signatures and are apt to occur again. Your ability to recognize them could lead to large trading gains. First, I will explain the candlesticks, then apply this theory to analysis of the graph. The candles are shown on the Dow chart that follows the explanation.

BULLISH ENGULFING

The bullish engulfing is most significant when it occurs after a prolonged downtrend. The stock or index has been selling off sharply. On the day of the bullish engulfing, prices often will start the day by falling. However, strong buying interest comes in and turns the market around.

Bullish Engulfing

The bullish engulfing is named thus because this candle surrounds or engulfs the real body of the previous one. When I discuss this candle with college students enrolled in my stock market course, I call it "Pac-Man" because, like the video game character, it "eats" the candle before it. The bullish engulfing represents a reversal of supply and demand. Whereas supply has previously far outstripped demand, now the buyers are far more eager than the sellers. Perhaps at a market bottom, this is just short-covering at first, but it is the catalyst that creates a buying stampede.

When analyzing the bullish engulfing, always check its size. The larger the candle, the more significant the possible reversal. A bullish engulfing that consumes several of the previous candles speaks of a powerful shift in the market.

THE HAMMER

This hammer marks a reversal off a bottom or off an important support level. On the day of the hammer, prices decline.

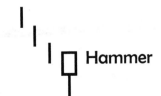

They hit bottom and then rebound sharply, making up all the ground—and sometimes more—compared to where the sell-off started. The candle shows that the buyers have seized control. A bullish candlestick on the following day confirms this analysis.

THE DOJI

If you were to learn only one candle by name, this would have to be the one. A "common" doji, as I call it, is shaped like a cross.

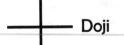

A doji has no real body. What it says is that there is a stalemate between supply and demand. It is a time when the optimist and pessimist, amateur and professional, are all in agreement. This market equilibrium argues against a strong uptrend or downtrend continuing, so a doji often marks a reversal day.

Therefore a doji in an overbought or oversold market is often very significant. The opening of the next day should be watched carefully to see if the market carries through on the reversal. Note, a candle with a very small real body often can be interpreted as a doji.

GRAVESTONE DOJI

The gravestone doji occurs far less frequently than the common one, but gives an even clearer signal. At the top of an extended move, it says the bulls tried to move the market higher and couldn't do it. The stock, or in this case the index, cannot sustain the probe to new high ground. It opens and closes at the exact same level creating the appearance of a gravestone.

Gravestone Doji

BACK TO THE DOW JONES CHART

During the period the chart illustrates, the Dow Jones Industrial Average went sideways in a broad trading range between 10000 and 11000. I have placed only one moving average on the chart, the 50-day. A 50-day moving average describes the intermediate trend, and when it moves sideways like it does here, you can also be sure it describes a market in a sideways consolidation pattern.

Despite the sideways movement, there were many good trading opportunities, both long and short. The first came in early March when the Dow peaked just below 11000. All round numbers represent key support and resistance in the major averages, and this top was no exception. The candle formed was a gravestone doji. Note

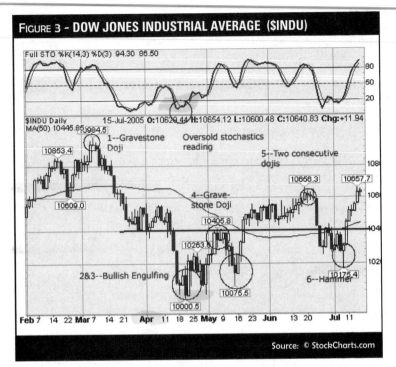

FIGURE 3 - DOW JONES INDUSTRIAL AVERAGE ($INDU)

Source: © StockCharts.com

the long upper shadow and the absence of a real body. This combination signalled that the bulls did not have the strength to push the Dow through the 11000 mark. Over the next month the Dow retreated nearly 1000 points, finally bottoming right at 10000.

The late April bottom at 10000 is marked by a bullish engulfing candle. Immediately before the bullish engulfing, note the three very large back candles which saw the Dow drop nearly 500 points in three days. That left it substantially oversold as shown by the stochastics indicator that reveals an oversold reading when it goes below 20 (above 80 is overbought). An oversold market can be described as one which has gone down too far, too fast.

The bullish engulfing candle was very large, adding to its significance. It implied that with the Dow able to hold 10000, the shorts were covering, buying interest had emerged at this level, or both. While the Dow didn't soar higher in the coming day, neither did it drop below 10000 again. By early May it rallied back to resistance near 10400. Note how a horizontal line can be drawn across the chart to mark this resistance level and how its role as both support and resistance alternated during the six-month period.

The minor uptrend brought the Dow back to 10400. Traders looking for the Dow to stall at this level did not have long to wait. Here's a small test of what you've learned so far. Can you name the candlestick that helped mark the peak at this time? If you said a gravestone doji, you get high marks.

The gravestone doji candle led to another small down-wave in the Dow. This was part of a secondary bottom that saw the index bottom well above 10000, closer in fact to 10100. Note there is a candle you have seen before—the bullish engulfing.

From 10075 the Dow advanced over the next month to a peak just below 10600. For almost a month, in what must have seemed like an eternity for traders, the Dow vacillated in an excruciatingly narrow range between 10400 and 10600. When it finally got beyond resistance at 10600, it formed three doji-like candles in a row. (The candles are doji-like because they have very small real bodies). These dojis showed that the bulls and bears were at a stalemate. After a lengthy uptrend they indicated that the bulls lacked the buying power to move the market higher. Not surprisingly, a strong sell-off ensued.

The decline ended well above 10000 this time, finding a bottom at 10175. The candle that formed here can be interpreted as a hammer, despite the very small upper shadow. The hammer candle occurred after the Dow had found support near 10250 for several days. On the day of the hammer, a dramatic news event sent prices sharply lower in the morning, but then the selling pressure dried up. By late afternoon, prices had turned positive as can be seen from the small white real body. The hammer led to a subsequent rally that lifted the Dow several hundred points in two trading days, taking it right back into the 10400 to 10600 range of resistance it had been in the previous month.

SUMMARY

I find it intriguing that the same candlestick patterns repeat continuously. All in all, there are about 100 candles patterns with which you can become familiar. Of these, 21 candles recur frequently enough and are significant enough that you should be able to spot them by name. Knowing their names allows you to spot them more easily and assess their implications. When faced with the need for a quick decision during the heat of trading, the trader who can name these 21 candles has a distinct advantage over one who can't.

LESSON 2

JAPANESE CANDLESTICK CHARTING

21 CANDLES EVERY TRADER SHOULD KNOW BY NAME

In the previous section of this book, I showed how certain key candlesticks were able to identify every major trend reversal in the Dow Jones Industrial Average for a period of several months. It is vital for trading success, I argued, to recognize candlesticks and assess their implications.

Candles are vital to trading because they identify possible reversals in trend. Failure to spot these key candles can lead to costly trading errors. Why should you be able to identify these candles? Because they can make you money!

CANDLES 1-4

THE FOUR DOJIS
SHOW STOCKS THAT
HAVE STALLED

If you were to ask me which of all the candlesticks is the most important to recognize, I would answer unhesitatingly — the doji. On a daily chart, the doji often marks the beginning of a minor or intermediate trend reversal. Fail to recognize the doji's implications, and you run the risk of buying at the top or staying far too late in a trade and leaving substantial profits on the table.

There are four types of dojis—common, long-legged, gravestone and dragonfly. All dojis are marked by the fact that prices opened and closed at the same level. If prices close very near the same level (so that no real body is visible or the real body is very small), then that candle can be interpreted as a doji.

After a long uptrend, the appearance of a doji can be an ominous warning sign that the trend has peaked or is close to peaking. A doji represents an equilibrium between supply and demand, a tug of war that neither the bulls nor bears are winning. In the case of an uptrend, the bulls have by definition won previous battles because prices have moved higher. Now, the outcome of the latest skirmish is in doubt. After a long downtrend, the opposite is true. The bears have been victorious in previous battles, forcing prices down. Now the bulls have found courage to buy, and the tide may be ready to turn.

What I call a "common" doji has a relatively small trading range. It reflects indecision. Here's an example of a common doji:

A "long-legged" doji is a far more dramatic candle. It says that prices moved far higher on the day, but then profit taking kicked in. Typically, a very large upper shadow is left. A close below the midpoint of the candle shows a lot of weakness. Here's an example of a long-legged doji:

When the long-legged doji occurs **outside an upper Bollinger band** after a sustained uptrend, my experience says you should be extremely vigilant for the possibility of a reversal. A subsequent sell signal given by an indicator such as stochastics typically is a very reliable warning that a correction will occur.

A "gravestone doji," as the name implies, is probably the most ominous candle of all. On that day, prices rallied, but could not stand the altitude they achieved. By the end of the day, they came back and closed at the same level. Here's an example of a gravestone doji:

Gravestone Doji

Finally, a "dragonfly" doji depicts a day on which prices opened at a high, sold off, and then returned to the opening price. In my experience, dragonflies are fairly infrequent. When they do occur, however, they often resolve bullishly (provided the stock is not already overbought as shown by Bollinger bands and indicators such as stochastics). Here's an example of a dragonfly doji:

Dragonfly Doji

When assessing a doji, always take careful notice of where the doji occurs. If the security you're examining is still in the early stages of an uptrend or downtrend, then it is unlikely that the doji will mark a top or a bottom. If you notice a short-term bullish moving average crossover, such as the four-day moving average heading above the nine-day, then it is likely that the doji marks a pause, and not a peak. Similarly, if the doji occurs in the middle of a Bollinger band, then it is likely to signify a pause rather than a reversal of the trend.

As significant as the doji is, one should not take action on the doji alone. Always wait for the next candlestick to take trading action. That does not necessarily mean, however, that you need to wait the entire next day. A large gap down, after a doji that climaxed a sustained uptrend, should normally provide a safe shorting opportunity. The best entry time for a short trade would be early in the day after the doji.

The chart of the Disk Drive Index ($DDX) shows three of the four dojis just described and gives some guidance on how to effectively interpret this candle, depending on where it occurs in a trend. The Disk Drive Index consists of 11 stocks in the computer storage and hard drive businesses. Therefore this index's performance usually correlates highly with the Nasdaq Composite. In March, the $DDX hit a peak of 125.06 and then a prolonged sell-off in conjunction with the overall market in general and tech stocks in particular. Also, note how in early May the $DDX traded sideways for several days, finding support or buying interest at the mid-97 level with resistance or selling pressure near the psychological barrier of 100.

Finally, the buyers were able to overwhelm the sellers and the $DDX pierced 100. Note on this day, the four-day moving average penetrated the nine-day. The 4-day moving average and the nine-day both began to slope upward. That pattern suggested an uptrend was beginning. The four-day moving average going above the nine is a bullish moving average crossover. While I wouldn't trade on this very short-term signal in isolation, it provides a useful confirmation that the immediate trend is up.

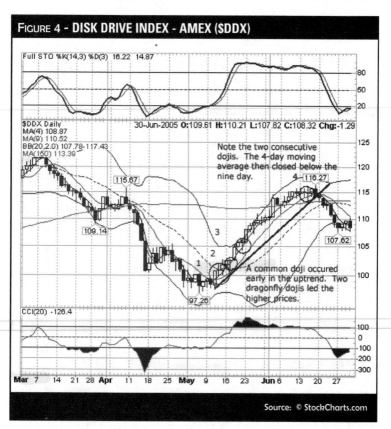

FIGURE 4 - DISK DRIVE INDEX - AMEX ($DDX)

The next day, a common doji appeared (labeled "1"). While a doji should always be noted, this one was early in the trend. The previously described "rule of two" also says to wait another day before taking trading action. The following day was positive.

Two days later a dragonfly doji appeared ("2") with prices closing at their highs. Again, a dragonfly doji often resolves positively as did this candle. Three days after that ("3") a second dragonfly doji occurred. This one was more worrisome since it came after a substantial advance and was close to the top of a Bollinger band. However, the uptrend continued.

By early June, the $DDX was trading close to 115. It had rallied nearly 20% off its early May low. Whereas during the core of the uptrend, there had been several large white candles indicating bullish enthusiasm, now the real bodies of the candles turned small showing caution on the part of buyers. Always observe the size of the candles in your analysis.

In mid-June, two consecutive dojis ("4") appeared on the chart. The first was a common doji; the second was closer to a long-legged variety. For those traders in a long position, extreme vigilance was now warranted. Substantial profits were there for nailing down in the $DDX. The index was stalling; the bulls and bear were stalemated.

In the two days after the dojis appeared, the $DDX struggled to move higher without much success. On the second day, the candle turned dark showing selling pressure. Note also that the four-day moving average penetrated down through the nine-day, the first time this had happened since the uptrend began in early May.

The subsequent slide in the $DDX was not dramatic. However, the trader who failed to heed the dojis' warning surrendered a large portion of his or her profits. Dojis should not be assessed mechanically. However, after a strong trend in either direction they often mark major turning points. Always recognize the doji when it occurs, and be prepared the next trading day to take appropriate action.

The one kind of doji not found in the $DDX chart is the grave-stone doji, already seen in the chart of the Dow Jones Industrial Average. Candlestick names typically are very colorful, and this one is no exception. If you are a bull, the gravestone doji should sound ominous and you should always be prepared to take rapid action on its appearance. When it occurs after a prolonged uptrend, and the upper shadow penetrates through the upper Bollinger band, the candle takes on added significance.

To review, a gravestone doji occurs on a day when prices open and close at the same level. During the session, however, prices move sharply higher, but the bulls cannot sustain the advance. This trading action leaves a long upper shadow on the chart. If the gravestone doji does not serve as a key reversal day, it certainly will mark a resistance area that normally will stall an advance for several sessions. In either case, the trader often is prudent to nail down profits after its appearance.

The chart of airline stock AMR Corp. (AMR) is a classic example of why it's vital to recognize the gravestone doji by name. AMR bottomed at $9.80 in late April. In early June, it had advanced nearly 40% and was probing the $14 area. On June 17, it opened at $14 and shot up to a peak of $14.95. Notice how a large part of the upper shadow pierced through the Bollinger band. But traders did not like the altitude that AMR was flying at and stock closed unchanged for the day. The session created a long-legged doji, a warning that the bulls were not able to maintain control.

Traders who required additional evidence that a reversal had occurred did not need to wait long. Notice, how the four day-moving average crossed below the nine day. A trendline break also occurs shortly after this crossover, suggesting AMR's flight path was now lower. Traders who ignored these signals paid a high price. By the end of June, AMR was probing $11, not far from where the rally began. This was one round trip that could have been avoided by assessing the implications of the gravestone doji.

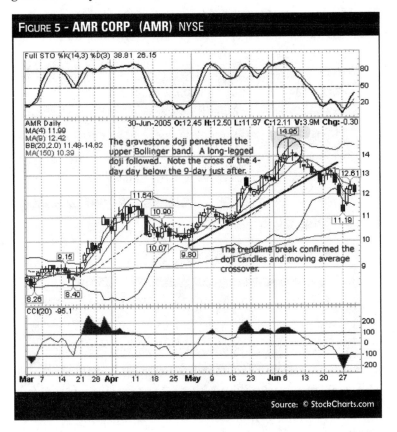

FIGURE 5 - **AMR CORP. (AMR)** NYSE

Full STO %K(14,3) %D(3) 38.81 26.15

AMR Daily   30-Jun-2005 O:12.45 H:12.50 L:11.97 C:12.11 V:3.9M Chg:-0.30
MA(4) 11.99
MA(9) 12.42
BB(20,2.0) 11.48-14.62   The gravestone doji penetrated the
MA(150) 10.39   upper Bollinger band. A long-legged
    doji followed. Note the cross of the 4-
    day day below the 9-day just after.

14.95

11.64

10.90   12.61

10.07   The trendline break confirmed the
9.80   doji candles and moving average
    crossover.

9.15

8.40

8.26

CCI(20) -95.1

Mar 7   14   21   28   Apr   11   18   25   May   9   16   23   Jun 6   13   20   27

Source: © StockCharts.com

CANDLES 5-6

HAMMER & HANGMAN CANDLESTICKS SIGNAL KEY REVERSALS

The doji candle probably is the single most important candle for the trader to recognize. Not far behind in value are hammer and hangman.

It is easy to confuse these two candlesticks because they look identical. Both the hangman and hammer have a very long shadow and a very small real body. Typically, they have no upper shadow (or at the very most, an extremely small one). To be an official hammer or hangman, the lower shadow must be at least twice the height of the real body. The larger the lower shadow, the more significant the candle becomes.

How can you tell the two candles apart? The hangman candle, so named because it looks like a person who has been executed with legs swinging beneath, always occurs after an extended uptrend. The hangman occurs because traders, seeing a sell-off in the shares, rush in to grab the stock at bargain prices. To their dismay, they subsequently find they could have bought the stock at much cheaper levels. The hangman looks like this:

On the other hand, the hammer puts in its appearance after a prolonged downtrend. On the day of the hammer candle, there is strong selling, often beginning at the opening bell. As the day goes on, however, the market recovers and closes near the unchanged mark, or in some cases even higher. In these cases, the market potentially is "hammering" out a bottom. Here is an example of a hammer candle:

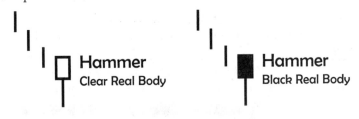

As with all candles, the "rule of two" applies. That is to say, a single candle may give a strong message, but you should always wait for confirmation from another indicator before taking any trading action. It may not be necessary to wait an entire trading day for this confirmation. When it comes to the hangman, for example, confirmation may be a gap down the next day. With the hammer, a gap opening with gathering strength as the day wears on may be all that is necessary to initiate a trade from the long side. Both hangman and hammer may appear in an up day (clear real body) or a down day (black real body).

I will start with the hammer. In my experience, when a hammer candle appears in the chart of one of the major averages, it is always a signal worth noting. This is particularly true when it has come after a steady and prolonged sell-off.

The chart of the Nasdaq Composite ($COMPQ) shows the value of the trader recognizing the hammer candle. From March to late May, Nasdaq was in a steep downtrend, having declined from almost 2100 to just below 1900. Right above the price chart, is another technical tool I frequently use, the Price Relative to $SPX. SPX stands for the S&P 500, so this chart compares the performance of Nasdaq to the S&P. Note that the thick line had

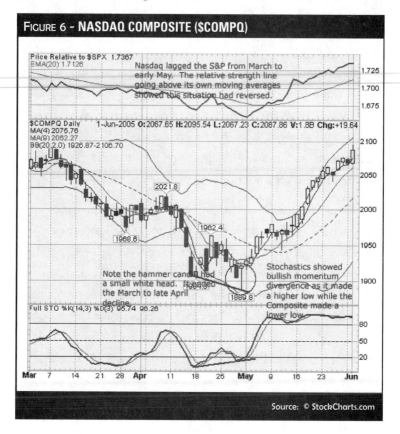

FIGURE 6 - NASDAQ COMPOSITE ($COMPQ)

Price Relative to $SPX 1.7367
EMA(20) 1.7126

Nasdaq lagged the S&P from March to early May. The relative strength line going above its own moving averages showed this situation had reversed.

$COMPQ Daily 1-Jun-2005 O:2067.65 H:2095.54 L:2067.23 C:2087.86 V:1.8B Chg:+19.64
MA(4) 2075.76
MA(9) 2062.27
BB(20,2.0) 1926.87-2106.70

2021.8

1962.4

1968.6

Note the hammer candle had a small white head. It ended the March to late April decline.

1889.8

Stochastics showed bullish momentum divergence as it made a higher low while the Composite made a lower low.

Full STO %K(14,3) %D(3) 96.74 96.26

Source: © StockCharts.com

a downward slope throughout the period of the chart and that it was under the thin line which was the 20-day moving average. That tells the trader that Nasdaq was under performing the S&P throughout the entire period.

The hammer candle occurred on the final day of April. On this day, the Composite breached 1900 intraday, but the bears did not have the power to close it under that psychological support level. Instead, the Composite closed slightly positively on the day, hence the small white head at the top of the candle.

In itself, the hammer gave a powerful warning that Nasdaq was reversing course. The alert trader might take a long position in a leading Nasdaq stock or an ETF (Exchange Traded Fund) such as the QQQQ on the next trading day when the Composite bullishly followed through on the previous day's action. On the second trading day after the hammer, the four-day moving average crossed above the nine-day and both began to slope higher, another bullish sign. Shortly thereafter, the Price Relative broke out above its own moving average, and for several weeks Nasdaq became the market leader instead of the laggard.

Additional technical confirmation of the hammer came from the behavior of the stochastics oscillator. Stochastics compares the behavior of price relative to its long-term price trend. It is a rapidly moving indicator which gives timely buy and sell signals. In this case, stochastics demonstrated bullish momentum divergence as marked on the chart. Bullish divergence occurs when price goes lower, but the stochastics oscillator rose. After the hammer, stochastics gave its first buy signal in roughly two weeks. The buy signal occurred as both %K and %D broke above 20 on the stochastics scale.

From that time onward, throughout the entire month of May, Nasdaq was off to the races. The Composite rallied roughly 200 points, from below 1900 to nearly 2100. The hammer candle was the technical signal that it was time to be long on the Nasdaq.

The candle opposite of the hammer is called hangman. When I have taught candlesticks in college stock market classes, students have easily become confused between the two. This is because they look exactly alike. The key difference is where they occur in a chart. The hammer occurs after a long decline when the market is oversold. In contrast, hangman puts in its appearance near the end of an uptrend when the market is overbought.

There are times when a hangman candle can look a great deal like the dragonfly doji. Such is the case with Forest Labs (FRX). In April, FRX had gapped down sharply from the $38 area when it announced below expectation earnings. Forest bottomed at $32.46 and in conjunction with strength in the pharmaceutical stocks began a gradual move higher. On the day of the hammer, it recovered to a peak of $40.76, butting up against strong resistance in the $40 to $42 area formed in February and March.

As shown in the chart on the following page, the hammer candle occurred outside the Bollinger band, a sign the stock was very overbought. I have also placed the CCI indicator on the chart. On this indicator, +100 is overbought and +200 highly overbought. Note that when the hammer candle occurred, CCI was well over 200 and was beginning to trend downward. Stochastics gave the same message as it gave a sell signal after having reached over-bought levels.

The hangman at the mid-June $40.76 point was indeed the profit-taking signal in FRX. The next day the stock opened just above $40 and slid persistently during the day, reaching a low of $37.60 before recovering. A simple trendline drawn from the $32.46 low confirmed that it was time to exit the position. The trendline was broken the next trading day. CCI also dipped below the +100 level, giving a sell signal on this indicator. When a candlestick, indicator, and trendline all give the same message, it is time to listen. While FRX went sideways rather than sharply down after the hangman, a position in the stock was dead money.

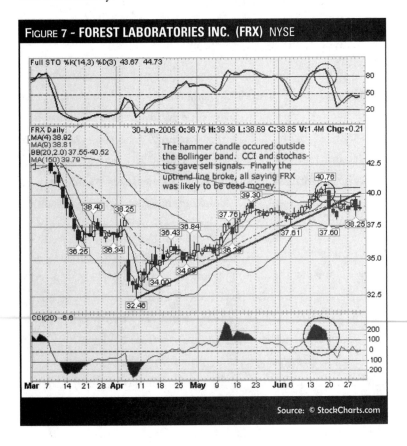

FIGURE 7 - **FOREST LABORATORIES INC. (FRX)** NYSE

CANDLES 7-8

BULLISH AND BEARISH ENGULFING CANDLES SPOT TREND CHANGES BEFORE THEY TAKE PLACE

If the doji wins the race as the most important candle to recognize, and hammer/hangman is a close second, then the "engulfing" candle places third. Whereas the doji and hammer/hangman are single candles, the engulfing pattern consists of two consecutive candles.

The engulfing candle must completely consume the real body of the previous candle. Because stocks have fewer gaps than commodities, an engulfing candle may violate this rule very slightly by being just above or below the top or bottom of the previous candle. In most cases, you should interpret this as an engulfing pattern. If you or your children are in the age group to remember the early video game Pac Man, you can think of the engulfing candle as being similar to the hero of that game in that it eats or consumes the previous candle.

A bullish engulfing candle occurs after a significant downtrend. Note that the engulfing candle must encompass the real body of the previous candle, but need not surround the shadows. Below is an illustration of a bullish engulfing candle:

A bearish engulfing candle occurs after a significant uptrend. Again, the shadows need not be surrounded. Below is an illustration of a bearish engulfing candle:

The power of the engulfing candle is increased by two factors—the size of the candle and the volume on the day it occurs. The bigger the engulfing candle, the more significant it is likely to be. A large bullish engulfing candle implies that the bulls have seized control of the market after a downtrend. Meanwhile, a large bearish engulfing implies that the bears have taken command after an uptrend. Also, if volume is above normal on the day when the signal is given, this increases the power of the message.

A good example of a bearish engulfing candle ending a rally is found in Avid Technology (AVID), a maker of video editing software. In early March the stock peaked in conjunction with the S&P 500 and Nasdaq Composite just above $68. A few days later, when it was trading at $62, it made an acquisition and was punished severely. Intraday, the stock was off nearly $5 and left a large gap between approximately the $60 and $62 level on the chart. Note also the large volume spike on that day. As we shall see later in this book, gaps in candlestick theory are called "windows," and create resistance to further price movement.

AVID eventually bottomed in late April at $47.64 and began to recover. By mid-June it was back above $60 and trading into the window it had created the day of the acquisition. That in itself should have made any long traders cautious on AVID. Another

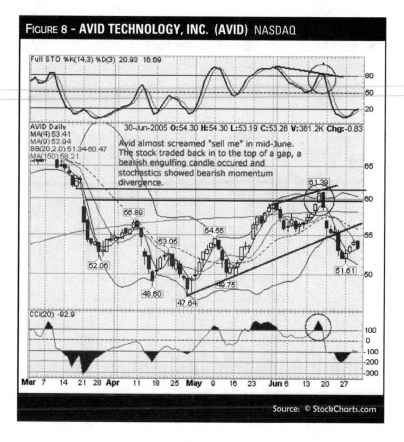

FIGURE 8 - **AVID TECHNOLOGY, INC. (AVID)** NASDAQ

Source: © StockCharts.com

reason for prudence, however, was that it was overbought. It was outside the Bollinger band. In addition to being in overbought territory on stochastics, there was also bearish momentum divergence. The day after the bearish engulfing candle, immediately after the stock topped at 61.39, it then gapped down. Stochastics and CCI gave clear sell signals and the trendline from the late April low was broken soon after. AVID retreated to near $51 before finally going outside the Bollinger band and becoming oversold, then staging a modest recovery.

The Utility TXU Corp (TXU) provides a good example of a bullish engulfing candle. From a low just under $60 in January, TXU

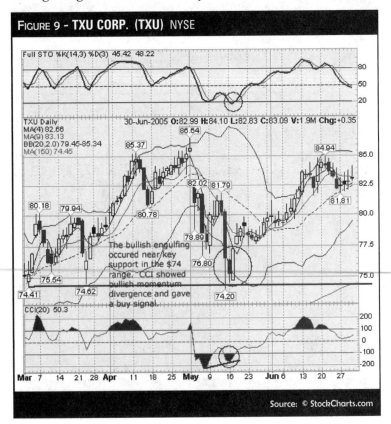

FIGURE 9 - **TXU CORP. (TXU)** NYSE

Source: © StockCharts.com

had a spectacular run to $86.64 by May before pulling back. Readers should note the strong support that existed between approximately $73 and $74, a level the shares did not did go below from February on.

In a single day in early May, TXU went from just over $80 down to support at $74. Note the long lower shadow that probed outside the Bollinger band on this session. Although this candle does not meet the requirements of a hammer (the shadow is not double the real body), traders should still pay close attention to long shadows, especially in areas of support. These shadows suggest that there is buying interest at that level.

Note also the bullish divergence on the CCI indicator that was recovering from oversold levels. Traders needed to wait two additional days for the bullish engulfing candle. But when it did come after the bottom of $74.20 it was a highly reliable signal. The candle was fairly large as the stock moved almost $2.50 on the day. CCU subsequently recovered to near $85, just below the previous highs.

CANDLE 9

DARK CLOUD COVER WARNS OF IMPENDING MINOR TOPS

The candlestick we will next explore is called "dark cloud cover." It is a close relative of the bearish engulfing, but is not quite as negative in its implications. Still, the appearance of this candle should be a warning to the trader to protect profits in a position. It also suggests that you should watch a stock as a possible short candidate in the trading days ahead.

The dark cloud cover candle occurs after a strong uptrend. A series of ascending candles is ultimately capped by a final white candle. At this point, the stock or index seems technically healthy, and the bulls may be lulled into a sense of false complacency.

On the day of the dark cloud cover, the stock opens above the previous day's high. For a true dark cloud cover to emerge, therefore, the stock should **gap above the upper shadow** of the previous white capping candle. At the opening bell on this trading day, it seems like the uptrend will continue.

As the day wears on, however, the bears wrest control. On the dark cloud cover day, the stock closes **at least halfway** into the previous white capping candle. The larger the penetration of the previous candle (that is, the closer this candle is to being a bearish engulfing), the more powerful the signal. Traders should pay particular attention to a dark cloud cover candle if it occurs at an important resistance area and if the end-of-day volume is strong. Below is an example of a dark cloud cover candle:

Dark Cloud Cover

Film and digital camera maker Eastman Kodak (EK) provides an example of the dark cloud cover. The stock traded as high as $33 in April, immediately before it released earnings and its second quarter forecast. When earnings came out in mid-April, the shares were changing hands at just above $30. Results were below expectations, the stock dropped precipitously on their release, gapping down to $27.16 and over the next several days were falling as low at $24.40. As we shall see when gaps are explored, the trader should now anticipate resistance between $27.16, the low end of the gap, and just above $30, the upper end.

Over the next month and a half, EK began a grudging recovery, regaining $27, backing off, and then finding consistent support at $26. The shares then broke out forming four consecutive white candlesticks and reaching a high of $28.19. While the third candlestick was not large, if the four candles were combined into one, it certainly would have been.

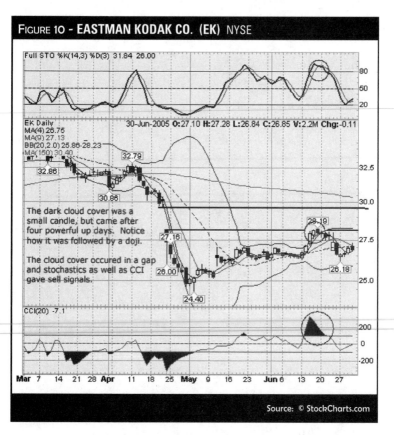

FIGURE 10 - EASTMAN KODAK CO. (EK) NYSE

When the dark cloud cover emerged after the high of $28.19, traders should have been wary. While this candle was relatively small, it retreated half-way back into the previous white candle. The next day a doji appeared, emphasizing the resistance near $28. EK then retreated toward the $26 level before finding support and rallying. While the dark cloud cover is not as potent a reversal candle as bearish engulfing, its appearance in the chart should be respected.

CANDLE 10

THE PIERCING CANDLE IS A POTENT REVERSAL SIGNAL

The dark cloud cover and piercing candles are like bookends. Whereas the dark cloud cover warns that an uptrend might be coming to an end and is thus a signal to take profits on long trades, a piercing candle indicates that a downtrend may be about to reverse and shorts should be covered.

The first thing to look for in spotting the piercing pattern is an existing downtrend. With daily candles, the piercing pattern often will end a minor downtrend (a downtrend that often lasts between five and fifteen trading days). The day before the piercing candle appears, the daily candle should ideally have a fairly large dark real body, signifying a strong down day. Here is an example of the piercing candle: In the classic piercing pattern, the

Piercing

next day's candle gaps below the lower shadow, or previous day's low. I find with stocks (in comparison to commodities), however, that the gap very is often below the previous day's close, but not less than the previous day's low.

On the piercing day, the candle comes back into and closes **at least halfway** into the real body of the prior day. If it does not come at least halfway back, then the candle is not a piercing candle and needs to be called by a different name. (The candle is "on-neck" if it closes at the prior day's low, "in-neck" if it closes slightly back into day one's real body, and "thrusting" if it closes substantially into the real body, but less than halfway.) In addition, the previous day's candle cannot totally make up the ground lost in day one, otherwise it would be a bullish engulfing.

Here are a few other points on the piercing candle. The closer it is to becoming a bullish engulfing candle, the more positive it is, and thus the greater the possibility of a reversal. Second, take particular note of the piercing candle if it occurs at an important support level. Third, if volume is strong on the piercing day, then the candle gains added significance.

An interesting example of a piercing candle is found in the chart of Avici Systems (AVCI), a VOIP or Voice Over Internet Protocol play. In mid-April, AVCI had bottomed near $3.70 for several days, creating a short-term basing formation. Toward the end of the month, it created a gap between approximately the $4.15 and $4.50 area, and then retreated to $4.16. Note the long lower shadow of the day the $4.16 bottom was made. Large lower shadows often serve as support areas. This one was doubly significant because it held the very upper end of the gap or window created several days earlier.

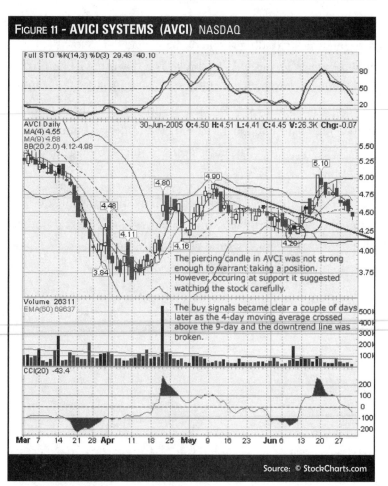

FIGURE 11 - AVCI SYSTEMS (AVCI) NASDAQ

The piercing candle in AVCI was not strong enough to warrant taking a position. However, occuring at support it suggested watching the stock carefully.

The buy signals became clear a couple of days later as the 4-day moving average crossed above the 9-day and the downtrend line was broken.

Source: © StockCharts.com

AVCI then advanced from $4.16 to $4.90 in mid-May, topping out just below round number resistance at $5. From there the stock went into a minor decline of 21 trading days, finally bottoming at $4.20. Note that at this level AVCI was at an important support created by the $4.16 low and was still above its late April gap.

The piercing candle appeared at support two days later. It was not a large range day and was accomplished on low volume. A trader who observed it might have made a mental note and watched with interest the trading action of the second day. Now the trend became much clearer. AVCI broke the downtrend line off the $4.90 high. It went back above its four and nine day moving average which gave a buy signal. Eventually, AVCI ran to $5.10 in mid-June before topping. Even if the trader had purchased at $4.50 and sold a few days later near $5, the percentage gain was substantial.

The piercing candle is a less powerful signal than the doji or bullish engulfing. Nevertheless, it is potent. Make a mental note to include it in your analysis the next time it occurs in a stock you own or are watching.

THE THREE CANDLE EVENING AND MORNING STAR PATTERNS SIGNAL MAJOR REVERSALS

By this point in *21 Candlesticks*, you should be able to spot several reversal candles. Many times, only one candle is necessary to put a trader on high alert that a reversal may be happening. A doji candlestick, whether it occurs after a long uptrend or downtrend, indicates that supply and demand are in equilibrium and that the recent trend may be ending.

Several major reversal patterns consist of two candlesticks. A bullish or bearish engulfing candle often signals a trend's conclusion. This two-candle pattern is also relatively easy to spot.

The evening star and morning star are, in my experience, harder patterns for the eye to discern. The reason for this is simple— because both patterns consist of three candles, these candles must be perceived **as a group**. However, once you've identified one of these patterns, then your job is pretty much over. Unlike most other candle formations, no further confirmation is needed. The evening and morning star are complete in and of themselves, so

the trader should strongly consider taking trading action immediately upon their appearance.

The **evening star** pattern occurs during a sustained uptrend. This
is my nursery rhyme for the evening star: *"IF YOU SEE THE
EVENING STAR, A TOP OFTEN IS NOT VERY FAR."*

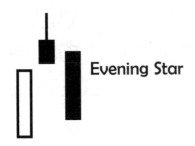

Evening Star

On the first day we see a candle with a long white body.
Everything looks normal and the bulls appear to have full control
of the stock. On the second day, however, a star candle occurs.
For this to be a valid evening star pattern, the stock must gap
higher on the day of the star. The star can be either black or white.
A star candle has a small real body and often contains a large
upper shadow.

The star communicates that the bulls and bears are involved in a
tug of war, yet neither side is winning. After a sustained uptrend,
those who want to take profits have come into balance with those
eager to buy the stock. A large upper shadow indicates that the
stock could not sustain its probe into new high ground. A potential reversal has been signaled.

On the third day, a candle with a black real body emerges. This
candle retreats substantially into the real body of the first day.
The pattern is made more powerful if there is a gap between the
second and third day's candles. However, this gap is unusual,

particularly when it comes to equity trading. As such, it is not a required part of the pattern. **The further this third candle retreats into the real body of the first day's candle, the more powerful the reversal signal.** Because the third day affirms the star's potentially bearish implications, no further confirmation is needed.

Continental Airlines (CAL) provides a good illustration of the evening star formation. The shares bottomed in late April as the stock created a hammer candle. The bottom was deceptive—the next day, the hammer was followed by a bearish engulfing and that candle was in turn succeeded by a large white candle. CAL rallied up close to its previous high of $13.36 of mid-April, backed off, and then soared. The shares completed an ascending triangle breakout on high volume and reached a peak of $15.60 in early June.

The evening star pattern is circled on the chart on the next page. On the first day, there is a reasonably large white candle. The second session sees a gap higher, indicated by the top of the black candle being somewhat higher than the white candle before it. Note the large upper shadow on this candle, indicating that CAL was not able to sustain prices above $15. The upper shadow occurred entirely above the top Bollinger band, indicating that CAL was substantially overbought.

On the third day of the formation, prices closed well back into the range of the first day, the final requirement of the evening star. Daily stochastics and CCI gave sell signals during this session also suggesting that the top for CAL was in. Note, how much earlier these signals were than the broken uptrend line that lagged the evening star by almost two weeks. And remember my trader's rhyme, "if you see the evening star, a top often is not very far."

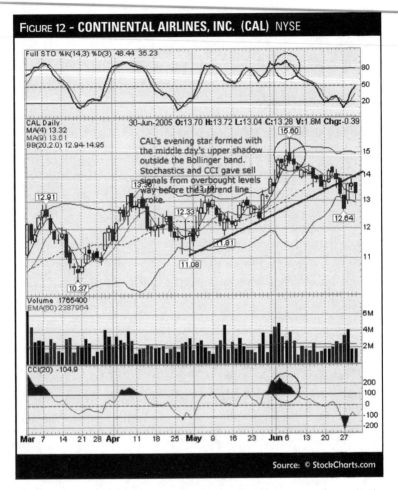

FIGURE 12 - **CONTINENTAL AIRLINES, INC. (CAL)** NYSE

CAL's evening star formed with the middle day's upper shadow outside the Bollinger band. Stochastics and CCI gave sell signals from overbought levels way before the uptrend line broke.

Source: © StockCharts.com

Having explored the evening star in detail, we need say little more about the **morning star** formation because it is the exact opposite of the evening star. It occurs in a downtrend and starts with a large black candle. On the second day, a star forms on a gap. The third day completes the reversal by closing well into the real body of day one.

Pharmaceutical giant and Dow Jones Industrial Average component Merck (MRK) experienced a long-term downtrend. In

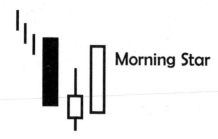

Morning Star

2001 the shares peaked near $100 and began a steady decline that took the shares to the mid-$40's in late 2004. Then the news hit that a key drug of Merck, VIOXX, increased the risk of heart attack and stroke. The headlines caused the stock to lose more than a third of its market capitalization in late September and continue to its rock bottom low of $25 in November.

From there, Merck began a very gradual recovery that saw the stock peak at $34.95 in early April. If you noticed that $25 and $35 were round numbers and reflected that these are both option strike prices, you've seen an important pattern.

After reaching $34.95, MRK went sideways for several weeks and then hit a secondary peak of $34.79 in early May. From here, MRK went into a prolonged slide reaching a low of $30.12 (notice again the $5 interval) in late June, rallying slightly and then testing a slightly lower low of $29.90 in early July.

The second low was revealing in a number of ways. First, as shown by the stochastics and CCI oscillators, there was bullish momentum divergence as price was lower, but stochastics and CCI itself were higher. The test of the lower day was also the second candle of the three-candle morning star formation.

Note, that on the first day there is a large dark candle. The middle day is not a perfect star, because there is a small lower shadow, but

the upper shadow on top of a small reall body gives it a star qual-
ity. The third candle is a large white candle that completes the
reversal. Note how the third candle recovered nearly to the highs
of the first day and occurred on strong volume. Also observe the
buy signal generated by stochastics on the day of the Morning
Star. After this candle, Merck bounced higher reaching a peak
near $32 several days later. The Morning Star, true to its name,
led to Merck's prospects brightening considerably.

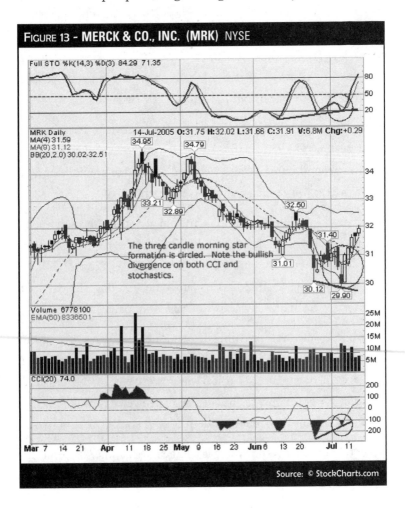

FIGURE 13 - **MERCK & CO., INC. (MRK)** NYSE

CANDLE 13

THE SHOOTING STAR
CAN WOUND

C andle theory identifies four kinds of stars: morning, evening, doji, and shooting. I now want to focus on the shooting star.

The shooting star can appear only at a potential market top. If you are looking at a daily chart, then it is possible that this candle will warn of a reversal in the minor uptrend. Since a minor uptrend typically lasts between six and fifteen days, the swing trader should be very alert if the minor uptrend is mature.

If a shooting star occurs after a candle with a large real body, typically it is that much stronger a warning because it shows that the price cannot sustain high levels. The day the shooting star occurs, the market ideally should gap higher (although with stocks rather than commodities, this gap is sometimes not present).

The stock should then rally sharply. At this point, it appears as though the longs are in complete control. Sometime during the day, however, profit taking ensues. The stock closes near the unchanged market, as shown by a small real body. Therefore a shooting star has a small real body and a large upper shadow. Typically, there will be either no lower shadow or a very small one. Here is a graphic representation of a shooting star candle:

Shooting Star

The small real body shows that the bulls and bears are at war with each other. Whereas the bulls had been in control during the uptrend, the two sides are now evenly matched.

The Semiconductor Index provides a clear example of why it is important to pay attention to the shooting star candle. The semis bottomed with the rest of Nasdaq in late April at 376.64. On that day, the $SOX broke support at 380 intraday, but then rallied strongly to close within the previous range. Note the hammer-like candle (it has a small upper shadow so is not a classical hammer) and long lower shadow.

From here, the $SOX commenced a strong rally that lifted the index nearly 64 points or approximately 17% in 24 trading days to the 440 level. At this point, both Nasdaq and the $SOX hit resistance. The $SOX tried to break 440 on six separate occasions, but was unable to do so. Finally it retreated to just below 420 and began another rally back toward resistance.

Toward the end of June, it broke through 440 intraday, briefly approaching important resistance (not shown on this chart) near the 450 level where it had stalled twice before in November 2004

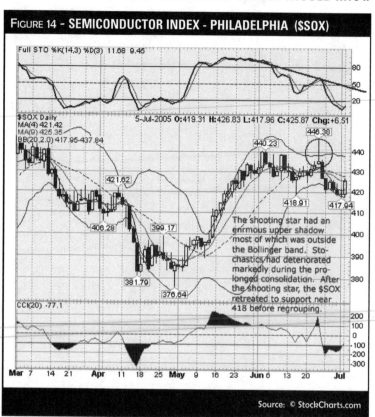

FIGURE 14 - SEMICONDUCTOR INDEX - PHILADELPHIA ($SOX)

The shooting star had an enormous upper shadow, most of which was outside the Bollinger band. Stochastics had deteriorated markedly during the prolonged consolidation. After the shooting star, the $SOX retreated to support near 418 before regrouping.

Source: © StockCharts.com

and March 2005. The candle that formed was a shooting star. Note how the large upper shadow went above the upper Bollinger band and the small real body. The $SOX had tested important resistance and failed.

The next trading day, it sold off sharply, bearishly engulfing the real body of the star candle. The $SOX then retreated to support near 418. The trader who missed the implications of the shooting star would have needlessly held semiconductor stocks through a sharp decline. If you can accurately recognize the shooting star candle, then you'll have another important tool to assist you in spotting early signs of a reversal. The candle will warn of the end of a minor uptrend before trend following tools such as moving averages or MACD. Recognize the shooting star or suffer the slings and arrows of stock market misfortune.

CANDLE 14

THE INVERTED HAMMER INDICATES THE SHORTS MAY BE READY TO COVER

Below you will find an illustration of the inverted hammer candlestick:

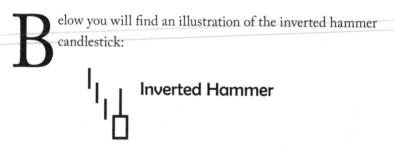

Inverted Hammer

The inverted hammer looks so familiar because it is identical in appearance to the shooting star discussed earlier. The difference is that the shooting star occurs at the end of a long uptrend. The inverted hammer, on the other hand, occurs after a significant decline has taken place.

If you examine the inverted hammer carefully, it hardly looks like a bullish candle. Prices opened low and then rallied strongly. By the close of trading, however, the stock has given back almost all of the day's gains. That leaves a small real body and a very large upper shadow. If anything, the candle looks bearish. The bulls could not sustain a rally, so the bears took the stock back toward its lows for the day.

So, why should this candle potentially set up an important reversal? My theory is that the inverted hammer often is a signal that shorts are beginning to cover their positions.

Here is my reasoning. Because the inverted hammer can only occur after a sustained downtrend, the stock is in all probability already oversold. Therefore, the inverted hammer signifies that traders who have held long positions in the security, most of whom are now showing large losses, often are quick to dump their shares by selling into strength. This will also serve to drive the stock back down.

With this candle, it is imperative to watch the next day's trading action. If the stock opens strongly **and remains strong during the day,** then a key reversal is likely in progress.

Not every inverted hammer will tune you in to this kind of short-covering situation. However, when you do see its appearance on a chart, then I suggest you do two things. First, check the short interest in the stock. Second, if that short interest is substantial, follow the stock closely the next trading day. Recognition of the inverted hammer may help you build market-beating profits.

National Information Consortium (EGOV) is a small cap stock that provides Web-building and software services to local, state, and the federal government. Prior to when this chart was taken, the stock had been in a narrow trading range with resistance just under $5.50 and support just over $4 for nearly six months.

EGOV peaked at $5.44 in early March and by late April had retreated to $4.13, a support level in the vicinity of its October

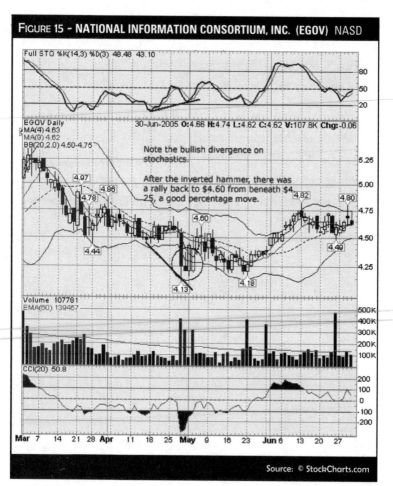

FIGURE 15 - NATIONAL INFORMATION CONSORTIUM, INC. (EGOV) NASD

lower Bollinger band. Although it formed a large black candle, note the large lower shadow as well, confirming that there was support just over $4.

The next day, EGOV formed an inverted hammer. The real body was small, and the upper shadow probed back toward the middle of the previous candle. The alert trader would have noticed that daily stochastics were bullishly divergent during this period.

Again, bullish divergence occurs when the momentum indicators make a higher low while price itself is making a lower low. Because momentum often proceeds price, it can be an important signal that a reversal is imminent.

That reversal came the next day, as EGOV formed a large white candle that reached approximately halfway back into the bottoming candle of two days previous. From there, EGOV traded into resistance at $4.60, backed off to a test of support, and then rallied sharply toward $5. The inverted hammer signaled the stock was close to a low.

CANDLE 15

THE HARAMI
IS PREGNANT WITH
TRADING POSSIBILITIES

W hen you visualize the harami candle, you should imagine that the first candle is like a mother and the second candle the child that emerges from its belly. That is where the name harami or pregnant comes from.

 Harami

The harami candle can occur both after an uptrend or downtrend. However, to keep this discussion clear, for the sake of example, I will assume a stock is in a uptrend. Immediately preceding the harami candle, there should be a large, real body dark candle. When this candle occurs, it is a bearish signal. The trend appears poised for a reversal.

A small real body candle appears within the larger real body. In my experience, the signal is more powerful if the second day's candle is near the middle of the trading range of the first.

The bullish harami candle can also occur in either bullish or bearish trends, but the colors are reversed: A large black body precedes a smaller white real body, and this gives out a bullish signal; it implies that the stock is poised to move upward. In either bullish or bearish haramis, the upper and lower shadows can be of any size, and theoretically could even go above the real body of the clear candle day. In practice, however, the harami day's shadows often are small and typically are contained well within the real body of the previous day's candle.

Always look carefully at the next day's candle—the one that follows the harami candle. Sometimes harami merely signifies that the stock is entering a period of consolidation (the shares will trade sideways). If, however, the stock you're examining after a bearish harami rallies the day after the harami candle takes place, then there is an increased likelihood that the shares have put in a minor bottom.

Polycom is a company that makes equipment for video-conferencing. As the 150-day moving average shows, the shares were in a long-term downtrend. In late May, PLCM hit a low of $14.80 and then rallied close to the resistance formed by the declining 150-day moving average at $17.99 in mid-May. From there, the shares fell rapidly, breaking the previous low of $14.80 in late June and continuing down to $13.97 at the beginning of July.

The day before the haramai appeared, PLCM fell from near the $15 range to just below $14. A large dark candle appeared on the chart, marked by volume, approximately 250% higher than normal.

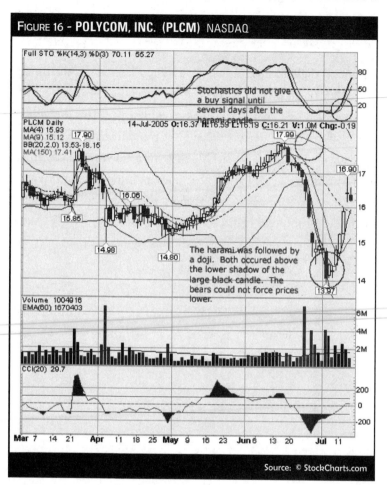

FIGURE 16 - **POLYCOM, INC. (PLCM)** NASDAQ

Source: © StockCharts.com

When the bullish harami appeared the next session (a large black real body followed by a smaller, clear real body), it held well above the lows of the previous day. The day after, a doji-like candle appeared, suggesting that the bears were not able to force prices any lower. From there, PLCM rallied nicely. By mid-month, the shares were testing $16, a gain of nearly 50% of the ground lost during the decline. Note that the stochastics buy signal from

61

oversold levels which confirmed the harami candle did not come until several days after the candlesticks signaled the reversal.

Although the harami candle is considered less potent than many of the key reversal candles, nevertheless it has substantial predictive power. If it occurs in a stock in which you have a position, then you should be alert to a change in trend from up to sideways, or from up to down. (If the stock is in a downtrend, then the harami candle can also warn of an impending period of sideways trading, or perhaps even an uptrend.) The next time you observe the harami candle, take heed, as it can provide you with a valuable tool to help you protect your profits.

THE FULL MARUBOZU IS A CANDLE WITHOUT SHADOWS

I n Japanese, the term marubozu means "close-cropped." Other common names for the marubozu include "shaven head" or "shaven bottom." Typically, the marubozu is a long candle that implies the day's trading range has been large. A marubozu candle lacks either an upper or lower shadow. On rare occasions it can lack both an upper or lower shadow. I am going to add a new term to candlestick terminology and call a long candle without either an upper or lower shadow a "full marubozu."

Marubozu

If you spend a lot of time at the trading screen, then you probably realize that a full marubozu is a very unlikely occurrence. Even after a strong up gap, most stocks experience a minor reversal, which leaves a small lower shadow. The same is true for the down gap. In addition, if a stock has moved sharply higher during the day, day traders often seek to nail down profits toward the end of the session. This creates a small upper shadow. Conversely, if a stock has sharply declined, then some short sellers will tend to cover before the close of trading. Because of this, stocks rarely close on their absolute low. In these cases there will be a small lower shadow.

When a full marubozu occurs, or one that is very close to full, it is very well worth noting. If it is a white candle, then it signals extreme conviction among buyers. Conversely, if it is a dark candle, then it indicates sellers were eager to flee. As always, you should pay careful attention to the next day's trading to see if there is follow through. A full or nearly full marubozu implies that there is strong buying or selling interest depending on the color. If there is follow-through early the next day, the stock is likely to trend in that same direction for the next few sessions. That awareness can be important for the trader.

The chart on the opposite page shows a stock that forms many nearly full marubozu candles: Amerada Hess (AHC) an oil company. Why does Amerada form so many marubozu or close to marubozu candles? Because trading in the stock correlates very closely with the price of crude oil. When oil is down, the stock sells off, usually falling consistently during the day. The reverse is true when oil rises.

As shown by the 50-day moving average that is sloping higher and below the share price, AHC was in a strong uptrend during this period. In less than a two-month period there were eight candles that were close to full marubozu. Five of these candles were bullish (clear real body). If one had bought any time after

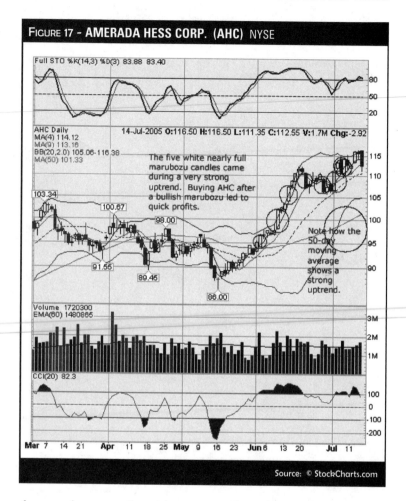

FIGURE 17 - AMERADA HESS CORP. (AHC) NYSE

The five white nearly full marubozu candles came during a very strong uptrend. Buying AHC after a bullish marubozu led to quick profits.

Note how the 50-day moving average shows a strong uptrend.

Source: © StockCharts.com

the maurbozu candle within two trading days in all cases, the trade would have been profitable. That is because the marubozu signaled a strong thrust in the trend often after a short period of consolidation.

The full marubozu usually is not considered a major candlestick. In my opinion, however, it should be added to this category. Although it is infrequent, this candlestick tends to be significant when it occurs.

CANDLES 17-18

HIGH WAVE AND SPINNING TOP EXPRESS DOUBT AND CONFUSION

Here is an interesting question, which candle is most opposite of the marubozu? Since the marubozu can be either white or black, the correct answer here cannot be another marubozu candle. Instead, opposite candles should include both spinning tops and high waves. I've provided you with an illustration of both of these candles below.

Spinning Top   High Wave

Why should these candles be considered opposites relative to the marubozu? When a marubozu candle occurs, it shows a great deal of conviction on the part of the market. A black marubozu portrays a very weak market in which the sellers are eager to exit and willing to get out of their positions at almost any price. Meanwhile, a white marubozu portrays the opposite situation, where buyers are willing to pay higher and higher prices to enter the stock.

In contrast, spinning tops and high wave candles denote situations where the market is having difficulty coming to a consensus on a security's value. They portray a market in which uncertainty and indecision prevail. Neither the buyers nor the sellers have a clear sense of which direction the market will head. The forces of supply and demand are equally balanced.

What is the difference between the spinning top and the high wave? In the spinning top, the shadows are relatively small and the candle has a very small range. When combined with low volume, traders may be expressing disinterest.

A high wave candle, on the other hand, portrays a situation where there is an active tug of war between the bulls and the bears. This candle shows a market that has lost a clear sense of direction. If it occurs on high volume, then it indicates the market's general confusion about the direction prices are headed.

Zimmer Holdings (ZMH) is a company that makes artificial joints used in such operations as hip and knee replacements. Prior to this chart, the stock had been within a prolonged wide-swinging trading range with much of the action concentrated in the mid-$70 to mid-$80 range.

In late April, Zimmer peaked at $83.70 outside the upper Bollinger band and began a slow, rolling decline that brought it back to the lower Bollinger band in both mid-May and early June. At the June low, we can observe first a high wave candle and, on the next trading day, a spinning top. Note on the high wave the long upper and lower shadows. With its small real body, the candle is close to a long-legged doji. On the next trading session, the spinning top occurred. Both of these candles occurred near key support just above $75. Take note of the very light volume on both of these sessions. The volume was well below the moving average line.

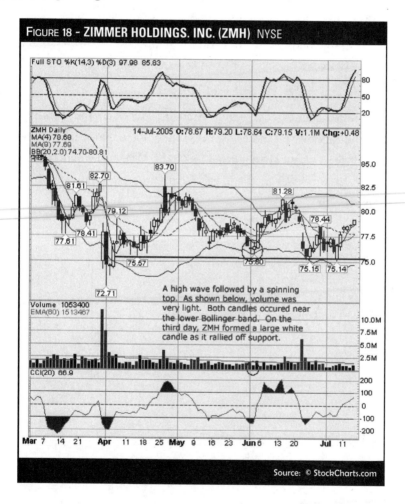

FIGURE 18 - **ZIMMER HOLDINGS. INC. (ZMH)** NYSE

A high wave followed by a spinning top. As shown below, volume was very light. Both candles occured near the lower Bollinger band. On the third day, ZMH formed a large white candle as it rallied off support.

Source: © StockCharts.com

Altogether, the technical indicators and two candles suggested that doubt and confusion existed in the minds of both buyers and sellers. Sellers were no longer motivated to exit the position, but buyers were not willing to step forward either. That situation changed the next day, when ZMH bounced sharply off support and formed a large white candle. On this session, Zimmer's future direction became clear in the short term: up.

ZMH ultimately recovered to a high of $81.28 before succumbing to profit taking and retreating to support near $75. But for the alert trader, the combination of candle signals and technical indicators pointed to a good opportunity.

As the old cliché goes, "when in doubt, stay out." The spinning top and high wave candles expressed doubt and confusion on the part of the market when it came to ZMH. When the market does tip its hand, however, the alert trader can seize a good trading opportunity.

CANDLE 19

THE OMINOUS CALL
OF THREE BLACK CROWS

The three black crows candle formation does not happen very frequently in stock trading, but when it does occur swing traders should be very alert to the crow's caw.

The candlestick's metaphor is three crows sitting in a tall tree. On the day the first black crow makes its appearance, the formation is most predictive if the first "crow"—or dark candlestick—closes below the previous candle's real body.

Two more long-bodied consecutive down days then ensue. On each of these days, it appears as if the stock wants to regain its former strength, as the stock opens higher than the close on the previous day. By the end of each session, however, the sellers regain control and the stock drops to a new closing low. Here is what the three black crows candlestick pattern looks like:

Three Black Crows

Note that the lower shadows on three black crows are small, or in some cases even nonexistent. Although three black crows is a complete pattern traders should always be alert to what happens on the fourth day after the pattern is formed. Since there has been intense selling throughout the pattern, the stock may be overextended to the downside. However, if the stock continues its negative pattern on the fourth day, then it is likely that the issue is going much lower.

The chart of Macromedia (MACR) was taken during the period the stock was acquired by Adobe Systems. During this time, MACR advanced from a late April low of $32.68 to an early June peak of $44.67. MACR then began to weaken, but found support just above the $42.50 level. Note the large black candle about 10 days into the decline. The lower shadow probed the $40 area, a key level of round number support.

Several days later, the first of the three black crows formed just above $40. The second crow broke decisively through the $40 level and the third crow took the shares down toward $38. By this time, MACR had fallen almost $4 in three days and on a very short term basis was substantially oversold. Oversold conditions may be relieved by a stock going either up or sideways, and in this case, MACR went laterally for the next four days. Eventually, the shares tested $35 before finding a short-term bottom.

Three black crows is an infrequent, but powerful candle formation. After observing its occurrence, the trader should likely resist the temptation to short since the issue is already short-term oversold. Rather, in most cases, the better approach is to watch the stock carefully. If it rallies weakly and then begins to falter, a short position can in most cases be initiated safely with a stop just above the high of the first black crow.

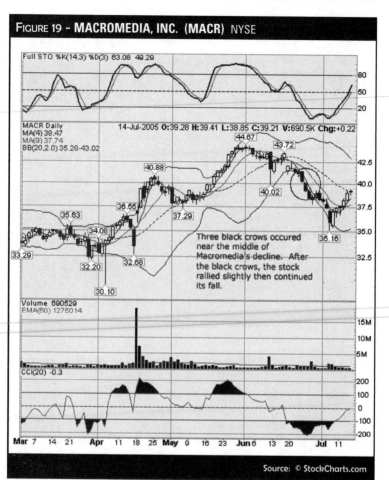

FIGURE 19 - **MACROMEDIA, INC. (MACR)** NYSE

Full STO %K(14,3) %D(3) 63.08 49.29

MACR Daily   14-Jul-2005 **O:**39.28 **H:**39.41 **L:**38.85 **C:**39.21 **V:**690.5K **Chg:**+0.22
MA(4) 38.47
MA(9) 37.74
BB(20,2.0) 35.28-43.02

44.67
43.72
40.88
40.02
36.55
35.63
37.29
34.08
33.29
35.16
32.20
32.68
30.10

Three black crows occured
near the middle of
Macromedia's decline. After
the black crows, the stock
rallied slightly then continued
its fall.

Volume 690529
EMA(60) 1275014

CCI(20) -0.3

Mar 7   14   21   **Apr**   11   18   25   **May**   9   16   23   **Jun** 6   13   20   **Jul**   11

Source: © StockCharts.com

THREE WHITE SOLDIERS CAN HELP YOU FIGHT FOR PROFITS

The bullish counterpart of three black crows is known as "three white soldiers" and is considered by some candle theorists as one of the most bullish candle patterns.

Three White Soldiers

The three white soldiers pattern is most potent when it occurs after an extended decline and a period of subsequent consolidation. When a particular stock posts a decline followed by a sideways movement, the appearance at that point of three white soldiers signals that higher prices are likely ahead.

The first of the three white soldiers is a reversal candle. It either ends a downtrend or signifies that the stock is moving out of a period of consolidation after a decline. The candle on day two may open within the real body of day one. The pattern is valid as long as the candle of day two opens in the upper half of day one's range. By the end of day two, the stock should close near its high, leaving a very small or non-existent upper shadow. The same pattern is then repeated on day three.

Although this candle pattern is very potent when a stock is at or near its lows, it should be regarded skeptically if it appears following a long advance in price. If you spot three white soldiers after a sustained rally, then it may mean a top is near. Be on the alert then for a reversal candle such as a doji or negative engulfing.

An extremely interesting example of three white soldiers occurred in the Biotech Index ($BTK). Two charts are necessary to illustrate a stunning reversal marked by three white soldiers.

The first chart focuses on the period from late December to early March. The Biotech index peaked along with the rest of the market in late December at 555. From there it began a steady downtrend. Note the very strong selling throughout this period.

There were several factors that tipped the alert analyst that the Biotech had changed course. The first was a hammer-like candle outside the Bollinger band. Note also the bullish divergence in stochastics on this second bottom. Bullish divergence occurs when price makes a lower low and the momentum indicator a higher low. The first of three white soldier candles also was a bullish engulfing, again providing strong evidence that the index was turning around.

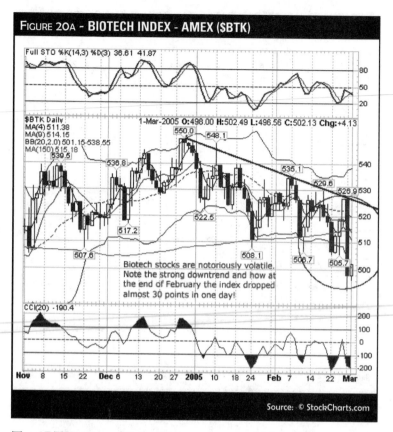

FIGURE 20A - BIOTECH INDEX - AMEX ($BTK)

Biotech stocks are notoriously volatile. Note the strong downtrend and how at the end of February the index dropped almost 30 points in one day!

Source: © StockCharts.com

The $BTK then rallied with a vengeance. This advance can be seen more clearly in the second chart. The decline from late December to early April took more than three months and saw the biotechs lose nearly 70 points. In three days, this group rallied to an intraday peak of 515.69, a recovery of 34 points or nearly half of the ground lost in three months.

Note how the biotechs went from one end of the Bollinger band to the other and stochastics from oversold to overbought. The three white soldiers had consumed a lot of buying power! After that the biotechs went sideways for most of the month, resolving the overbought condition.

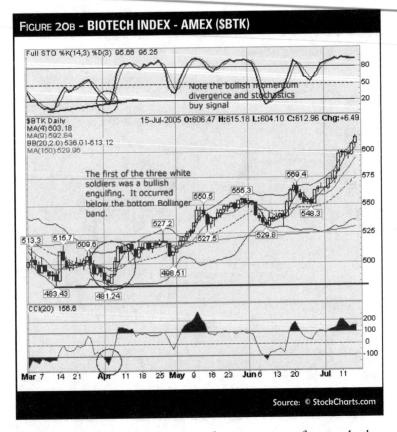

Figure 20B - BIOTECH INDEX - AMEX ($BTK)

Full STO %K(14,3) %D(3) 95.66 95.25

Note the bullish momentum divergence and stochastics buy signal

$BTK Daily   15-Jul-2005 O:606.47 H:615.18 L:604.10 C:612.96 Chg:+6.49
MA(4) 603.18
MA(9) 592.84
BB(20,2.0) 536.01-613.12
MA(150) 529.96

The first of the three white soldiers was a bullish engulfing. It occurred below the bottom Bollinger band.

569.4

555.3

550.5

548.3

527.2

527.5

529.8

513.3   515.7
509.6

498.51

483.43   481.24

CCI(20) 156.8

Mar 7   14   21   Apr   11   18   25   May   9   16   23   Jun 6   13   20   Jul   11

Source: © StockCharts.com

The three white soldiers pattern does not occur frequently, but as a swing trader you definitely should be on the lookout for it. These soldiers make great allies in your battle for swing trading profits.

CANDLE 21

TWEEZERS CAN HELP YOU PULL PROFITS OUT OF THE MARKET

In my experience, tweezers candles do not occur all that often in the stock market. However, when they do indeed take place, they are almost always significant.

What are tweezers candles?

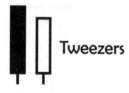 Tweezers

Candlestick theory recognizes both a tweezers top and a tweezers bottom. The tweezers formation always involves two candles. At a tweezers top, the high price of two nearby sessions is identical or very nearly so.   In a high priced stock there may be a few cents variation, and I believe it should still be considered a tweezers. At a tweezers bottom, the low price of two sessions that come in close succession is the same.

For simplicity, let's talk just about the tweezers bottom. In some instances, the tweezers bottom is formed by two real candlestick bodies that make an identical low. In other instances, the lower shadows of two nearby candles touch the same price level and the stock then bounces higher. A third possibility is that the lower shadow of one day and the real body of a nearby session hit the same bottom level.

Most traders are familiar with a double bottom or double top. For this formation to occur, the chart you're looking at should generally show at least fifteen trading days between the two tops or bottoms. The double top or bottom typically is a forecasting formation that applies to intermediate-term reversals.

In my mind, the tweezers pattern is analogous to a very short-term double top or double bottom. What the tweezers candles say is that prices held twice at the exact same level or very close to it. At the bottom, sellers were not able to push the stock lower. At the top, the bulls were not able to drive prices higher. Tweezers thus signify very short-term support and resistance levels.

Tweezers sometimes occur on two consecutive trading sessions. In these cases they are relatively easy to spot. However, they can also occur several sessions apart, say six or eight. (If they are spread further apart than that, then the formation is beginning to approach the double bottom or top described above.) When the tweezers occur consecutively, their forecasting value generally increases. Why? Well, in these cases a bullish or bearish move has been absolutely stopped in its tracks and is more likely to reverse.

As with any candles, swing traders should watch carefully the price action that occurs immediately after the tweezers candles. If the tweezers bottom is to be a meaningful reversal, then the low formed by the two candles should hold. If the bottom is penetrated, then prices are likely to descend to at least the next important support level. The opposite is true for a tweezers top. Burlington Northern Railroad (BNI) was a stock on fire as investors bid up much of the Dow Jones Transportation Average of which it forms a part. The stock ran from the low $46 range in early February to a peak of $56.28 in late March, a price that formed a peak for the stock. Burlington then formed a small head and shoulders top and then took a round trip right back to the $46 level in mid-April.

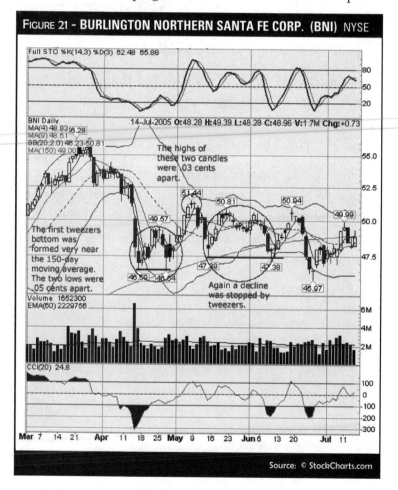

FIGURE 21 - **BURLINGTON NORTHERN SANTA FE CORP. (BNI)** NYSE

Source: © StockCharts.com

A tweezers bottom then marked the conclusion of the selling pressure. The first low occurred at $46.59. Eight trading days later, BNI tested $46.54, five cents lower then the first tweezers candle. Note the long lower shadows on both candles saying sellers were eager to step in and buy in this zone of support.

I have also included a 150-day moving average on the chart. Note that the moving average was sloping up. To define the long term trend, I typically put the 150-day moving average on the chart. When it is rising and below the share price, it provides support and often stops a correction particularly the first time it is tested.

From the mid-$46 range, BNI rallied to $51.62 on May 6 and $51.59 on May 9. These days were Friday and Monday, so they were consecutive. A tweezers top stalled the recovery and the shares again pulled back falling this time to a low just over $47.

Tweezers candles do not occur as frequently as other candles such as dojis. When they do arise, however, they generally give rise to high-probability trading opportunities. Recognize this candle formation and you'll have a much easier time extracting money from the market.

LESSON 3

INTEGRATING MULTIPLE CANDLESTICKS & INDICATORS

ROUND NUMBER RESISTANCE, CANDLESTICKS, AND INDICATORS

Thus far in this book, we have focused on the power of individual candlesticks or candlestick patterns. We have seen that certain individual candles such as the doji have the power to signal significant reversals in and of themselves.

Two candle patterns such as bearish engulfing, and three candle formations such as morning star, can mark entirely new directions in trend. These candles and candle patterns begin key reversals, often anticipating any other kind of technical evidence such as from indicators or trendlines.

A key variation in the one- to three-candle reversal pattern sometimes occurs in individual stocks or indices. There are times when the market stalls at key levels and goes sideways for what can seem to the trader like an interminable period. During this time, many of the 21 candlesticks I've asked you to learn by name occur. However, the balance between the bulls and the bears, between supply and demand, is so fine that neither side can win a decisive advantage. A bullish candle may be followed by a bearish one and that candle reversed in turn.

These sideway movements often occur at times of significant support or resistance. Resistance, you may remember, occurs when prices have risen to such a level that new buyers are reluctant to enter the market. Support emerges when the opposite occurs: sellers are exhausted and buyers must bid higher to enter a position.

Technicians identify resistance and support as coming from a large number of factors. Resistance may occur at a price level that has been hit many times before, from an important moving average such as the 50 or 200 day or from the top Bollinger band. It can also emerge when prices push up against the upper end of a channel or even when certain round numbers are reached.

Of these varieties of resistance, round-number resistance is the kind I find the most fascinating and potentially the most far reaching for making trading decisions. This resistance occurs when prices reach a certain whole number and then stall. Perhaps one of the most dramatic instances of this phenomenon was the inability of the Dow Jones Industrial Average to meaningfully penetrate the 1000 level for approximately 16 years from 1966 to 1982. But the alert trader will note this kind of resistance in virtually every stock and at every different price level.

For a low price stock, an even dollar amount will usually cause buyers to enter and for prices to stall. I often notice that the $5 and $10 levels are difficult to penetrate on the first or second try. After that, even $5 amounts such as $15, $20 and $25 are common prices at which stocks stall in their advance. One might imagine that when shares reach elevated price levels such as $60 or $70, that $1 would be such a small percentage change that it wouldn't make a difference, but I have seldom found that to be the case. When day trading, I always pay attention to round numbers. A stock may rise from say $41.20 at the open to $42.10 intraday. But before I jump on board, I will always want to make sure this penetration of $42 is going to last.

In gauging round number resistance with the major averages, some slight leeway is necessary. In the example below, I am going to analyze the 10700-price level that stalled the Dow Jones Industrial average for several months. One would not expect the Dow Jones, for example, to hit 10700 exactly on each day it tested that level. On some occasions it might fail at 10690 and at others penetrate 10700 and climb as high as 10750 intra-day. Occasionally, it might even close above 10700, although it is difficult for the index to sustain this altitude for more than a day or two.

The Dow Jones chart that I referred to is on the next page. In early July, the index hit a low of 10175 and rebounded sharply intra day. By the end of the session, the Dow had rebounded to close near 10300 and formed an enormous hangman candle. That candle was followed the next day by a large white candle that bullishly engulfed the trading range of the previous nine days and the rally was on. Several days later, the Dow reached a peak of 10696. That level is marked "1" on the chart shown on the next page.

At this time, there were few technical reasons to believe the Dow would not blow through 10700 and perhaps challenge 11000, a previous resistance level. But the very next candle

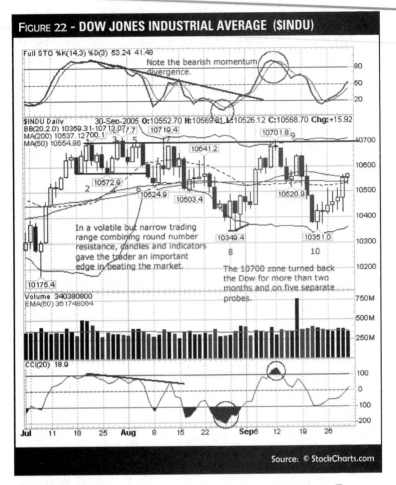

FIGURE 22 - DOW JONES INDUSTRIAL AVERAGE ($INDU)

Full STO %K(14,3) %D(3) 53.24 41.48

Note the bearish momentum divergence.

$INDU Daily   30-Sep-2005 O:10552.70 H:10569.81 L:10526.12 C:10568.70 Chg:+15.92
BB(20,2.0) 10359.31-107 13.077.7   10719.4
MA(200) 10537.12700.1
MA(50) 10554.86

10701.8

10641.2

10572.9

10524.9   10503.4   10520.9

In a volatile but narrow trading range combining round number resistance, candles and indicators gave the trader an important edge in beating the market.

10349.4   10351.0

8   10

The 10700 zone turned back the Dow for more than two months and on five separate probes.

10175.4

Volume 340380800
EMA(50) 361748064

CCI(20) 18.9

Jul   11   18   25   Aug   8   15   22   Sep6   12   19   26

Source: © StockCharts.com

(marked "2") dashed those hopes. Can you see why? Because it was bearish engulfing. It suggested that traders who bought between 10175 and 10500 were more than happy to nail down strong near Dow 10700.

For the next several days, the Dow waffled in a very narrow trading range. It found support in the 10560 zone, a level that had provided buying interest earlier in the month. Note how the two laterals lines drawn on the chart mark the bounds of a very narrow trading zone. This very constricted rectangle formation contained the Dow for several trading days as it vacillated between support and resistance.

Near the end of the month, the Dow again pressed up against resistance. At "3" for the first time, it closed above 10700 for the first time in this move, finishing the session at 10705.55. Again the bulls no doubt entertained hopes of a breakout and higher prices ahead. Once more, at "4," their hopes were dashed. Again, can you say why? The next candle was dark cloud cover as it opened slightly above the previous day's close and closed very near the low for the day.

But the Dow bulls were not yet ready to be deterred. Early the next month they again tested the 10700 level. This time a hangman candle formed at "5." Bears, or those looking to pin down profits, should have been watching the next day carefully. A hangman, after all, is a major reversal candle and it played its role to perfection. The next trading day at "6," a large bearish engulfing occurred, and that led to a sell-off that brought the Dow back to key moving average support near 10525.

But the Dow bulls were not yet exhausted. Two trading days later, the index made one last probe of the 10700 during this period. Except for the small lower shadow, the candle formed at "7," a near-perfect shooting star, another major reversal signal. Although the next day was a positive white candle, technicians should have been very suspicious because there was extreme bearish momentum divergence.

As you may remember, bearish momentum divergence forms when price hits a new or equivalent high, but the momentum indicator makes a lower high. Both the stochastics and CCI indicators had deteriorated markedly since the Dow had first probed 10700 several weeks earlier. Typically there will be bearish divergence after a long period of sideways action, a decline, and then the probing of old resistance. Traders should learn to be skeptical of the price action during these times. The technical maxim is momentum precedes prices, and it pays to be extra patient at these times before entering a trade on the long side.

At many junctures such as the one I have been describing, it always pays to look at as many technical factors as possible. Even for those with a short-term trading focus, a look at the weekly chart in addition to the daily is always instructive. In this case the weekly chart provides the trader with a great deal of additional insight.

The chart on the facing page is comprised of exactly the same data and indicators as the daily. Note what happened. After two large white candles, the Dow stalled. It formed a near-doji candle at Dow 10700, a clear signal that the strong advance from the 10175 level was running out of steam. The next week, a second doji-like candle appeared. This one was slightly more ominous than the first. Why? It was dark and just about bearishly engulfed the first.

Note also the message of the two momentum indicators immediately after the two dojis. Both gave sells signals. Stochastics said sell as %K crossed below %D above the overbought 80 level, and CCI echoed this message when it fell from above +100 to below +100.

Therefore, the final probe for this period should, based on almost all the technical evidence, have been regarded with great suspi-

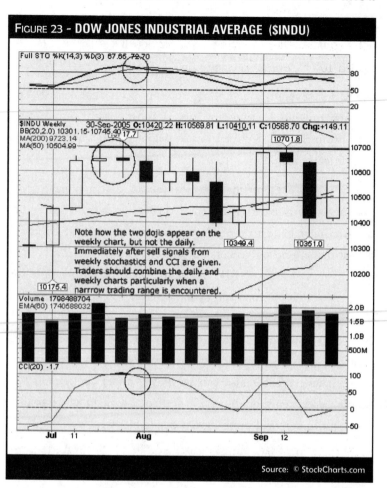

FIGURE 23 - DOW JONES INDUSTRIAL AVERAGE ($INDU)

Note how the two dojis appear on the weekly chart, but not the daily. Immediately after sell signals from weekly stochastics and CCI are given. Traders should combine the daily and weekly charts particularly when a narrow trading range is encountered.

Source: © StockCharts.com

cion. First, on the weekly chart a very large upper shadow was left, similar to the daily shooting star. Next, there was strong momentum divergence on the daily chart. Finally, the probe of 10700 occurred while both weekly CCI and stochastics were on sell signals.

Alert technicians recognized these signals in real time and the Dow retreated sharply over the next several weeks. A combination of using candlesticks, indicators and round number resistance would have saved the trader from buying at the wrong time or given back a large percentage of previously earned profits.

Let's return to the daily Dow chart. The index hesitated at 10500 for several days, finding support both near its 50- and 200-day moving averages and also at an important round number. From there it declined to just below 10350 where it scored a significant bottom.

Can you spot some of the technical factors that may have given the buyers confidence? First, the Dow had gone from one end of the Bollinger band to the other end. Second, note at point "8" how it made a near tweezers bottom on the last two days of the month scoring lows of 10321.42 and 10329.15. Third, note the long lower shadows on each of the three candles suggesting that buyers at these levels thought they were buying at bargain levels. Note also how both stochastics and CCI had become oversold and soon gave buy signals after the three long-shadowed candles. A small uptrend line also can be drawn under the second two candles, and even though there is not much data on which to base this trendline, it will often have predictive power.

From there, the Dow rallied back to just above 10700 at point "9." This rapid advance left the Dow overbought on both stochastics and CCI and again brought it back to the top of the Bollinger band. A long white candle was followed by a doji and then a large dark candle that implied 10700 resistance was not to be overcome anytime soon. If the doji had been more star-like, the three-candle formation would have been a classic evening star formation, again signaling an important reversal.

The Dow again retreated and found short-term support (point "10") right around the 10350 level just where the previous decline had halted. Soon the Dow was advancing, although it peaked below 10700 resistance.

Traders should note how during this period the 50- and 200-day moving averages were both flat and very tightly "bunched." This configuration occurs when the market enters a prolonged and near trendless sideways consolidation phase. During these periods where the bulls and bears are engaged in a tug of war but neither side can win, there can be intense volatility within the trading range. One of the few ways to make money during this kind of period is to recognize reversal signals virtually as soon as they occur. Combining candlesticks, indicators, and support and resistance should give you some of the essential tools to survive and even thrive in this kind of choppy market environment.

GAPS FROM
A JAPANESE
CANDLESTICK
VIEWPOINT

WHAT IS A GAP?

A gap is a hole in the chart. It occurs because on a particular day a stock opens or closes much higher or lower than on the previous session. The cause of a gap can be varied. Some common reasons for gaps are earnings announcements, important corporate news, or even large moves in the overall market at the opening of trading.

THE FOUR TYPES OF GAPS

The trader should be able to identify four different types of gaps: area (common), breakaway, continuation (measuring), and exhaustion.

An area gap occurs within a trading pattern such as a triangle, rectangle, or base. Typically, the area gap is of little significance.

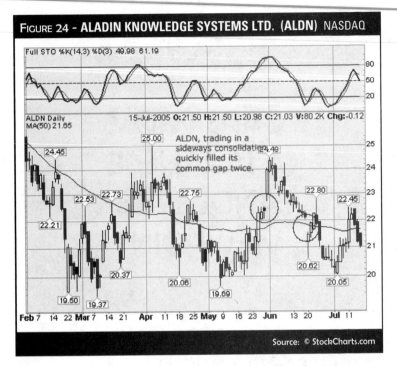

FIGURE 24 - ALADIN KNOWLEDGE SYSTEMS LTD. (ALDN) NASDAQ

Since area gaps often are filled quickly, they conform to traditional wisdom that gaps are filled. The stock Aladin Knowledge Systems (ALDN) shows two examples of area gaps. In both cases, these gaps were filled quickly.

A breakaway gap is an entirely different matter. The breakaway gap ends a consolidation pattern and happens as prices break out. Often, a breakaway gap occurs on very large volume, as the supply available within the consolidation pattern has been consumed and bidders who want to enter the stock must pay up for it. A genuine breakaway gap often will not be filled for weeks or months (if ever).

The chart of Conagra (CAG) shows a breakaway gap that occurred on enormous volume.

Note how the stock tried to rally back toward resistance at $25.44 on the end of the gap. It failed right below that level and left an enormous upper shadow. Volume on that day was about 350% high than normal levels. If the stock were to approach $25.44 again, it would face very strong resistance as all the buyers who had the chance to get out at close to breakeven would be tempted to do so.

A continuation gap occurs within a rapid straight-up movement. This type of gap is also known as a measuring gap because it usually occurs approximately halfway through the move.

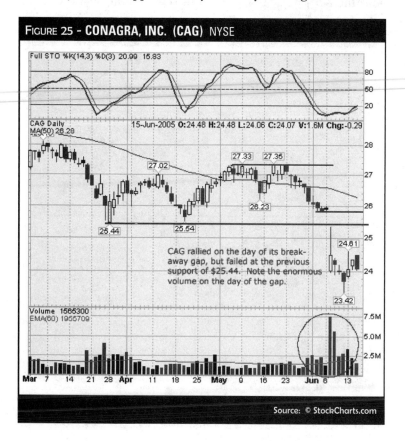

FIGURE 25 - **CONAGRA, INC. (CAG)** NYSE

CAG rallied on the day of its breakaway gap, but failed at the previous support of $25.44. Note the enormous volume on the day of the gap.

Source: © StockCharts.com

95

Continuation gaps may eventually be filled, but it should take some time to do so as the stock needs to first peak, reverse, and finally trend in the opposite direction.

A fascinating example of a continuation gap occurs in the chart of Brinter Intl. (EAT), a restaurant chain. The stock peaked just shy of the $40 level in March and hit a low of $33.19 in late April. After a snappy recovery, the stock closed at $36.95 on June 8. Note the move from $33.19 to $36.95 was $3.76.

The next day EAT gapped up on news that the company was boosting both its quarterly and full year earnings outlook. The

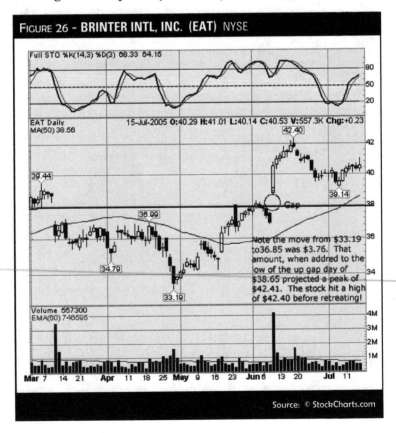

FIGURE 26 - BRINTER INTL, INC. (EAT) NYSE

Source: © StockCharts.com

stock opened at $39.25, backed off to $38.65, and closed over round number resistance at $40. A continuation gap typically takes place approximately halfway through the move. If you add the prior move of $3.76 to the low of the gap day, $38.65, the target becomes $42.41. The stock hit $42.40 several trading days later!

An exhaustion gap occurs at the end of a price move. If there have been two or more gaps before it, then this kind of gap should be regarded very skeptically. A genuine exhaustion gap is filled within a few days to a week.

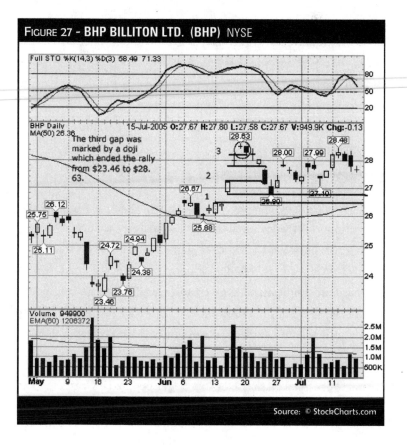

FIGURE 27 - **BHP BILLITON LTD. (BHP)** NYSE

Source: © StockCharts.com

BHP Billiton is an Australian mining stock that trades on the New York Stock Exchange. The company tends to form many gaps because the trading that takes place in Australia before the NYSE opens influences BHP's performance dramatically on that day.

In mid-June, however, note that BHP made an unusual number of gaps in a row, even for this stock. The third gap formed a doji and the stock reversed, filling the top and middle gap, but finding support at the bottom one. With gaps I often find that the "three strikes and you're out" rule applies. The third gap often is the final one.

When a trader sees a gap, he or she should immediately ask, "What kind of gap am I witnessing?" Often it will take some time to come to a final conclusion. What seems to be a breakaway gap, for example, may over the next several weeks be filled, and that filling may be an important catalyst to take trading action in the opposite direction.

CANDLESTICK THEORY ON GAPS

Candlestick theory, while less detailed about gaps, provides some important additional insights. Japanese theory does not distinguish between the types of gaps. Nor does it even use this term. Instead a gap is called a "window." Whereas a great deal of emphasis in candlesticks is given to reversal patterns, a window is considered a continuation pattern. In other words, trading is highly probable to continue in the same direction after the window as it did before it.

In his work on candlesticks, Steve Nison advises traders that typically they should trade "in the direction of the window." If a particular stock is declining when the window occurs, then it is highly probable that the decline will continue. If the stock is rising when the window occurs, then it should continue to rally.

Once a window has occurred, the pattern often forms into an important support and resistance area. If the window occurred in a downtrend, then on any subsequent rally the upper end of the window should turn back prices. If the window was created in an uptrend, then when prices rally the bottom edge of the window should be the lowest point of decline. Further, candle theory holds that the test of all open windows is likely. The key thing to examine is what happens on this test.

When the alert swing trader spots a window in a rising trend, he or she should expect, for a time, that the price will continue higher. Eventually, however, prices will reverse and will test the open window. On this test, prices should hold at the lower edge of the window, which is now important support. If, however, this support level is violated and selling pressure persists, then it is likely that the trend has reversed. The swing trader should now go short in the same way he or she would so if a horizontal support level had been breached.

In a downtrend, the opposite is true. After the initial window, the decline should continue. Eventually resistance, which is at the upper edge of the window, should be tested. If buying pressure persists and is able to move prices beyond this upper window, then swing traders should go long in the same way they would if a resistance level were overcome.

SYNTHESIS OF WESTERN WISDOM AND EASTERN INSIGHT

Combining Western wisdom and Eastern insight on gaps, what then are some key trading tactics you can take away? The principles below should be applied within the context of other chart messages such as moving averages, trendlines, and stochastics. That said, here are several trading principles based on gaps:

1. On spotting a gap in a daily chart, immediately question yourself as to which of the four kinds of gaps it is.

2. Generally, short-term trades should be in the direction of the gap. The larger the gap and the stronger the volume, the more likely it is prices will continue to trend in that direction.

3. If an area gap is identified, then the swing trader should look for a short-term peak. When prices begin to move back toward the gap, a trade may be placed anticipating the gap will be filled.

4. Upon identifying a continuation gap the trader should, other factors considered, buy quickly. The trader should then use the measuring principle, which applies to this gap, to identify the short-term target.

5. A breakaway gap also provides an immediate buy point, particularly when it is confirmed by heavy volume.

6. The third upside gap raises the possibility an exhaustion gap has occurred. Swing traders should look for the gap to be filled in approximately one trading week. If the gap or window is filled and selling pressure persists, then that issue should be shorted. If the gap is the third one to the downside, then traders should be alert for a buy signal.

Although gaps are powerful analytical tools, generally they should not be acted on in isolation. View the gap within the context of the other technical messages given by the chart. For a complete system of gap analysis, traders should apply both Western and Eastern concepts of gap analysis. Hopefully, this summary of gaps has filled in some holes in your knowledge of how to apply this technical analysis concept.

A CONCLUDING
CHALLENGE

Now that you have read *21 Candlesticks*, I have a challenge for you. Take a sheet of paper and see how many of the candlesticks you can name from memory. After you've done that, review the ones you missed until you can name all 21 by heart.

Next, go back and draw the candlestick diagrams next to the text. Again, see how many you can draw from memory. Go back and check your results against the earlier chapters of this book. Repeat this exercise until you can name and draw all 21 candles.

The benefit of this exercise will be that you will be able to recognize the 21 candles when they occur in trading situations. If you are a short term trader, this will help you immeasurably to pick up on key continuation and reversal patterns. If you trade intraday, you will be much more sensitive to changes in the ebb and flow of supply and demand as signaled by candles.

Good luck and good trading!

TRADING
RESOURCE
GUIDE

SUGGESTED READING

STRATEGIES FOR PROFITING WITH JAPANESE CANDLESTICK CHARTS - DVD COURSE

by Steve Nison

What are Japanese Candlesticks and why should traders use them? This video workshop will help you understand and master this powerful tool with high impact results. Steve Nison is the premiere expert on Candlesticks in the world and now you can benefit from his expertise in the comfort of your own home. Filmed at a unique one-day seminar he gave for a select group of traders you'll find discover:

- The most import candle patterns

- Using the power of candles for online trading

- Combining Western technical indicators with candlestick charts for increased profits

- Reducing risk with candlestick charts

- Swing and day trading with candlestick charts and so much more

It's an incredible opportunity to have the foremost expert guide you to trading success now at a great savings.

$695.00 Item #BC106x2434165

▲ ▲ ▲ ▲ ▲ ▲

THE CANDLESTICK COURSE

by Steve Nison

In *The Candlestick Course*, Nison explains patterns of varying complexity and tests the reader's knowledge with quizzes, Q&As and intensive examples. In accessible and easy-to-understand language, this book offers expert instruction on the practical applications of candlestick charting to give every level of investor a complete understanding of this proven, profitable and time-tested investing technique. Straightforward answers quickly clarify this easy-to-use charting method. This guide will allow you to recognize and implement various candlestick patterns and lines in today's real-world trading environment – giving you a noticeable edge in your trading activities.

$65.00 Item #BC106x84668

REMINISCENCES OF A STOCK OPERATOR

by Edwin Lefèvre

Generations of investors have benefited from this 1923 masterpiece. Jack Schwager's new introduction explains why this account of Jesse Livermore, one of the greatest speculators ever-continues to be the most widely read book by the trading community. *"The best book I've read--I keep a supply for people who come to work for me."* - Martin Zweig

$19.95 Item #BC106x2116

▲ ▲ ▲ ▲ ▲ ▲

TO GET THE BEST PRICES ON ANY ITEM LISTED
GO TO WWW.TRADERSLIBRARY.COM

HIT AND RUN TRADING: THE SHORT-TERM STOCK TRADERS' BIBLE

by Jeff Cooper

Discover winning methods for daytrading and swing trading from the man who wrote the bible on short-term trading. Professional stock trader Jeff Cooper first released his original Hit & Run Trading Book almost a decade ago, taking the short-term trading world by storm. Now, he's back with a newly updated Hit & Run Trading Volume I. Jammed packed with a full arsenal of new tools and strategies to help day traders compete and survive in this fast-paced, volatile arena.

$100.00 Item #BC106x3156887

▲ ▲ ▲ ▲ ▲ ▲

**TO GET THE BEST PRICES ON ANY ITEM LISTED
GO TO WWW.TRADERSLIBRARY.COM**

Free 2 Week Trial Offer for U.S. Residents From Investor's Business Daily:

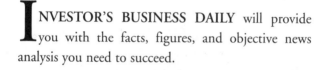

FREE 2 WEEK Trial Offer

INVESTOR'S BUSINESS DAILY

Power Processors Light Up Internet
Even When All The Lights Go Out

I NVESTOR'S BUSINESS DAILY will provide you with the facts, figures, and objective news analysis you need to succeed.

Investor's Business Daily is formatted for a quick and concise read to help you make informed and profitable decisions.

To take advantage of this free 2 week trial offer, e-mail us at customerservice@traderslibrary.com or visit our website at www.traderslibrary.com where you find other free offers as well.

You can also reach us by calling 1-800-272-2855 or fax us at 410-964-0027.

ABOUT THE AUTHOR

D r. Melvin Pasternak has studied and traded the stock market for more than 40 years, having made his first trade in 1961. For more than a decade he taught classes in technical analysis for TD Waterhouse and also instructed stock market classes at the college level for many years.

Dr. Pasternak holds both Ph.D. and M.B.A. degrees and writes a trading oriented newsletter called the *Swing Trader* at www.streetauthority.com.

Dr. Pasternak is a regular technical analysis commentator for CBC radio, Canada's national radio station. His stock-picking methods have been profiled in several newspaper articles.

He actively trades his own account where the methods described in this book form a key part of his decision making. In his best year, Dr. Pasternak multiplied his account several hundred percent and completed more than 80% of his trades profitably.

This book, along with other books, is available at discounts that make it realistic to provide it as a gift to your customers, clients, and staff. For more information on these long lasting, cost effective premiums, please call us at (800) 272-2855 or you may email us at sales@traderslibrary.com.